The History ....

The Rise and Fall of Pride Fighting Championships: A Legendary Era in MMA History

James Bren

Chapters

Introduction to *The History of Pride FC*

PRIDE Fighting Championships, known as Pride FC, was one of the most influential mixed martial arts (MMA) promotions in the history of the sport. Founded in 1997 by the Japanese company Dream Stage Entertainment (DSE), Pride FC introduced a new era of fighting that captivated MMA fans around the world. Its inaugural event took place at the Tokyo Dome on October 11, 1997, marking the beginning of a decade-long reign in the MMA world. Over the years, Pride FC would host more than sixty events, drawing millions of fans and viewers across many countries.

Pride FC's popularity was fueled by its focus on spectacle and entertainment, borrowing heavily from the traditions of Japanese professional wrestling. Unlike other MMA organizations, Pride FC made its events larger than life, with extravagant opening ceremonies, elaborate entrances for the fighters, and high-energy productions that set it apart from its competitors. The events often took place in massive sports stadiums, and Pride held some of the largest MMA events in history, including the Shockwave/Dynamite event in 2002, which set the record for the largest live MMA audience with over 91,000 people in attendance. Another notable achievement was the Pride Final Conflict 2003, which drew a crowd of more than 67,000 people. These monumental events helped solidify Pride FC's place as one of the most recognized MMA promotions worldwide.

A unique aspect of Pride FC was its unorthodox approach to matchmaking. Unlike modern MMA organizations, Pride did not strictly adhere to weight classes in most of its bouts. This led to the promotion of "freakshow" fights—matches that pitted fighters of wildly different sizes and skill levels against each other. A classic example of this was the match between sumo wrestler Akebono and former UFC fighter Bob Sapp, which garnered significant attention due to the stark contrast in their backgrounds and fighting styles. Another hallmark of Pride was its Grand Prix tournaments, which were single-elimination, one-night events where fighters from multiple weight classes competed for the ultimate prize. These tournaments were often thrilling and unpredictable, creating memorable moments for fans.

Pride FC's rule set was another factor that set it apart from other organizations. The rules were more permissive than the Unified Rules of Mixed Martial Arts, allowing techniques such as soccer kicks, stomps to downed opponents, and knees to the head. Additionally, the fights were held in a boxing-style ring, rather than the traditional octagon, giving the bouts a distinct feel. Matches began with a 10-minute opening round, followed by two 5-minute rounds, which added an extra layer of strategy to the competition. This blend of unique rules and high-octane action made Pride a favorite among hardcore MMA fans who appreciated the chaos and excitement that came with the fights.

However, despite its immense success, Pride FC faced significant financial troubles in the mid-2000s. In 2006, a scandal involving the company's alleged ties to the yakuza, the Japanese criminal syndicate, resulted in the loss of key sponsorship deals and television contracts. This financial turmoil forced DSE to sell Pride FC to Zuffa, the parent company of the UFC, in 2007. Under Zuffa's ownership, there were hopes of merging the two promotions, but these plans never materialized. By October 2007, Pride FC's operations were effectively shut down, and many of its top fighters were transferred to the UFC, signaling the end of an era for the organization.

Though Pride FC ceased to exist as a fight promotion, its influence continued to be felt in the MMA world. In 2015, Nobuyuki Sakakibara, a co-founder of Pride FC, went on to establish the Rizin Fighting Federation in Japan, with the goal of carrying on the same philosophy and excitement that made Pride so successful. Rizin, like Pride, is known for its large-scale events, fighter spectacle, and an emphasis on entertainment.

The story of Pride FC is one of immense success, unexpected scandals, and unforgettable moments. The organization's commitment to entertainment, its innovative rules, and its unforgettable fighters helped shape the modern landscape of MMA. Even years after its closure, the legacy of Pride FC remains a crucial chapter in the history of mixed martial arts. This book will explore the rise and fall of Pride FC, its most iconic fighters and fights, and its lasting impact on the sport we know today.

The Lasting Legacy of Pride FC in Mixed Martial Arts

As the story of Pride FC comes to a close, it's clear that its influence on mixed martial arts is far-reaching and everlasting. In its relatively short lifespan, the promotion changed the landscape of combat sports forever. The organization's commitment to spectacle, its innovative approach to matchmaking, and its rule set challenged the norms of traditional MMA organizations and set new standards for both athletes and promotions alike.

Pride FC's thrilling events, filled with high-energy fights, dramatic entrances, and larger-than-life personalities, captured the imagination of MMA fans around the world. The promotion's disregard for traditional weight classes, often matching fighters of vastly different sizes, became part of its charm and its unpredictability. The Grand Prix tournaments, which featured some of the most dramatic and exciting moments in MMA history, continue to be a hallmark of the sport's evolution.

The fighters who rose to prominence in Pride FC are forever etched in the annals of MMA history. Legends like Wanderlei Silva, Fedor Emelianenko, and Mirko Cro Cop not only defined an era of great competition but also helped elevate the sport into a mainstream global phenomenon. These athletes became household names, and their performances in the Pride ring helped to elevate MMA from a niche sport to one of the most widely watched forms of entertainment in the world.

While Pride FC may no longer exist, its legacy lives on in the organizations that followed, most notably the UFC. The acquisition of Pride by Zuffa in 2007 marked a pivotal turning point in the MMA industry, merging two of the biggest names in the sport and introducing a new era of global competition. The UFC continues to benefit from the fighters who made their names in Pride and the lasting impact of Pride's rule set, style, and culture.

Additionally, the influence of Pride FC is still seen today in promotions like Rizin Fighting Federation, which was founded by former Pride FC president Nobuyuki Sakakibara in 2015. Rizin has continued the tradition of high-energy, spectacular events that were a staple of Pride, ensuring that the spirit of Japan's greatest MMA promotion is not forgotten. Even as MMA continues to evolve, Pride FC's contributions to the sport remain a fundamental part of its history and development.

The rise, peak, and fall of Pride FC is a tale of triumph, scandal, and lasting influence. It shows how a passion for combat sports, paired with an innovative vision, can leave a mark on an entire industry. Pride FC's unique blend of entertainment and athletic competition helped shape the MMA landscape we know today, and the fighters, moments, and philosophy that defined the organization will continue to inspire future generations of fighters, fans, and promoters.

Part One: The Birth of a Giant – Pride FC's Formative Years (1997–1999)

Chapter 1: Pride Has Its Roots in Japanese Professional Wrestling (Puroresu)

In the 1970s, Antonio Inoki became a central figure in Japanese professional wrestling, or "puroresu," by founding New Japan Pro-Wrestling (NJPW). He introduced a new style of wrestling, which he called "strong-style," influenced by his training in Karate and Catch-As-Catch-Can. This style was much more intense than traditional wrestling, incorporating full-contact strikes, kicks, and realistic grappling techniques. Inoki's vision was to make wrestling appear more legitimate, blurring the lines between entertainment and real combat sports.

Inoki's strong-style emphasized a more realistic approach to wrestling, with intense strikes and a greater focus on grappling, all inspired by Catch Wrestling. Unlike the scripted, choreographed matches common in the West, Inoki's vision aimed to showcase the strength and toughness of his style by making it appear more like a genuine contest. His belief was that this form of wrestling was the "strongest" combat style, capable of standing up against other martial arts.

One of the most notable aspects of Inoki's NJPW was the introduction of "heterogeneous combat sports bouts" or Ishu Kakutōgi Sen. These were matches between Inoki's strong-style wrestlers and fighters from other martial arts, such as judo, kickboxing, sumo, and karate. While these matches still had predetermined outcomes, they were designed to showcase the real skills of each combat sport, leading to an exciting, unpredictable clash of styles. This idea of mixing various martial arts to find the strongest was a significant step toward the future development of mixed martial arts (MMA).

The most famous example of these cross-discipline matches was Inoki's 1976 fight against world boxing champion Muhammad Ali. This match, held in Tokyo at the Budokan Arena, became a pivotal moment in the history of combat sports. The fight was supposed to be a spectacle, but neither fighter could agree on the outcome, and the match evolved into a real fight, with both men giving their all. Despite the uncertainty and controversy, the match ended in a draw, but it helped popularize the idea of cross-discipline combat and blurred the boundaries between professional wrestling and real fighting.

The Inoki-Ali fight, though inconclusive, had a lasting impact on the world of combat sports. It proved that there was a genuine interest in seeing different combat styles clash, and it popularized the idea of bringing together fighters from various backgrounds. This fight, along with Inoki's push for stronger, more realistic wrestling, played a significant role in paving the way for the development of MMA.

Inoki's approach and vision of merging different combat sports set the stage for the creation of promotions like PRIDE FC. By the time the 1990s arrived, the idea of mixing martial arts into one unified competition was gaining traction. PRIDE FC, when it was founded, took inspiration from Inoki's philosophy of cross-discipline competition, and it was this groundwork that helped PRIDE rise to the top of the MMA world in Japan. Like NJPW, PRIDE focused on dramatic events, with a strong emphasis on the spectacle, and often pitted fighters from different disciplines against each other.

PRIDE FC wasn't the only promotion influenced by Inoki's ideas. His legacy also lived on in the formation of Rizin Fighting Federation in 2015. Founded by former PRIDE president Nobuyuki Sakakibara, Rizin took a page from Inoki's book by continuing to mix various combat styles and focusing on spectacular events that entertain fans while showcasing legitimate martial arts skills. Even today, Inoki's influence can be seen in how modern MMA events blend sports and entertainment.

Inoki's impact on professional wrestling and combat sports is undeniable. His work in NJPW and his vision for strong-style wrestling laid the foundation for mixed martial arts as we know it today. The cross-discipline matches he promoted helped to shift the focus of combat sports toward a more legitimate and competitive format, which would eventually evolve into the globally recognized sport of MMA. His belief in the power of different combat styles, and his desire to create more realistic matches, changed the world of fighting forever.

The Lasting Legacy of PRIDE FC in Combat Sports

PRIDE FC's influence on mixed martial arts (MMA) is undeniable, and its impact continues to resonate within the sport today. Founded in the late 1990s, PRIDE quickly became one of the most significant MMA promotions worldwide. With its origins rooted in Japanese professional wrestling, PRIDE combined athletic competition with dramatic spectacles that attracted millions of fans. The promotion's unique approach to combat sports, especially its integration of fighters from diverse martial arts backgrounds, set it apart from other organizations.

From its early years, PRIDE's focus on cross-discipline competition and larger-than-life events made it stand out in the world of combat sports. By mixing different martial arts and promoting intense, often unpredictable matchups, PRIDE helped shape the landscape of MMA as we know it today. Its rule set, which was more permissive than the Unified Rules of Mixed Martial Arts, allowed for moves like soccer kicks and stomps, adding an extra layer of excitement and brutality to the bouts. This unique style not only attracted hardcore fight fans but also casual viewers who were drawn to the spectacle.

The fighters who made their names in PRIDE, such as Fedor Emelianenko, Wanderlei Silva, and Mirko Cro Cop, became global superstars. These athletes, known for their diverse skills and toughness, contributed to the promotion's success. Their memorable performances in PRIDE events helped to elevate MMA to a mainstream sport, drawing attention from around the world. Many of these fighters later transitioned to the UFC, where they continued to make a significant impact on the global stage, cementing PRIDE's place in MMA history.

In addition to the fighters, the production values of PRIDE events helped to elevate the sport's appeal. The organization's focus on entertainment, including elaborate entrances, opening ceremonies, and spectacular fight cards, helped turn each event into a major spectacle. The dramatic flair of PRIDE's shows created an atmosphere that made fans feel like they were witnessing something truly special. This focus on spectacle, while still maintaining a commitment to real competition, played a significant role in the popularity of MMA in Japan and worldwide.

Despite its success, PRIDE FC eventually ran into financial trouble. A scandal involving ties between its parent company, Dream Stage Entertainment (DSE), and the yakuza led to the end of lucrative broadcasting contracts in Japan. In 2007, the promotion was sold to the owners of the UFC, leading to its eventual closure. However, even after PRIDE ceased to exist as a fighting promotion, its influence remained. Many of its fighters and staff went on to contribute to the development of other MMA promotions, such as Rizin Fighting Federation, which carries on PRIDE's legacy in Japan today.

The rise and fall of PRIDE FC serve as a reminder of how quickly the world of combat sports can change. While the organization may no longer be active, its contributions to the sport continue to be felt. The fighters, the production style, and the ruleset that PRIDE pioneered have all influenced modern MMA in significant ways. Whether through its emphasis on larger-than-life spectacles or its promotion of cross-discipline bouts, PRIDE helped shape the future of combat sports.

Looking back, PRIDE FC can be seen as a critical step in the evolution of MMA. It proved that there was an audience for a sport that combined the intensity of various martial arts with the entertainment value of professional wrestling. As the UFC took the reins of the MMA world, it was clear that PRIDE had left its mark on the global fight scene. The promotion's focus on high-energy events, unique matchups, and exciting fighters helped to popularize MMA, ensuring its place in the mainstream.

The legacy of PRIDE FC will never be forgotten. The organization's contributions to the growth of mixed martial arts helped to shape the sport into what it is today. Its dramatic rise, unforgettable moments, and eventual closure serve as a testament to the promotion's unique place in combat sports history. Even though PRIDE is no longer around, its influence lives on through the fighters who made their mark and the promotions that continue to draw inspiration from its legacy.

Chapter 2: The Evolution of Shoot Wrestling and the Foundations of PRIDE FC

The fight between Antonio Inoki and Muhammad Ali was more than a spectacle; it became a defining moment that inspired generations of wrestlers and martial artists. Among those deeply influenced were Inoki's students, who sought to continue his vision of blending realism and wrestling. Dissatisfied with the traditional professional wrestling style, these students left New Japan Pro-Wrestling (NJPW) to form the Universal Wrestling Federation (UWF). The UWF adopted a style known as "Shoot Wrestling," which was designed to resemble real combat while retaining predetermined outcomes. This stripped-back, more realistic approach captured the imagination of fans in Japan.

The UWF operated with great success, but it eventually closed its doors in 1990. Its successor, the Union of Wrestling Forces International (UWFi), launched in 1991 and quickly became a dominant force in Japanese wrestling. UWFi embraced Shoot Wrestling's philosophy, creating events that looked and felt closer to real fights. The promotion's main attraction was Nobuhiko Takada, a charismatic and skilled performer who became a superstar in Japan. Takada's matches showcased the popularity of shoot wrestling, proving that audiences were eager for this style of combat entertainment.

During the rise of UWFi, other organizations were also experimenting with realistic styles. Shooto, founded in 1985 by Satoru Sayama—better known as "Tiger Mask"—was a hybrid martial arts organization that combined various fighting styles. Shooto emphasized real competition, with fighters testing their skills against one another in unscripted bouts. Sayama's vision for Shooto set a standard for what would later evolve into modern mixed martial arts (MMA).

Another significant influence on PRIDE FC was Pancrase, established in 1993 by Masakatsu Funaki and Minoru Suzuki. Unlike most wrestling promotions of the time, Pancrase was entirely unscripted, emphasizing real fights between competitors. This commitment to authenticity helped Pancrase gain a loyal following and further blurred the lines between professional wrestling and MMA. Its success showcased the potential for combat sports that combined various martial arts disciplines, paving the way for future promotions like PRIDE.

In 1994, Satoru Sayama organized Vale Tudo Japan, a tournament inspired by Brazilian Vale Tudo and the Ultimate Fighting Championship (UFC). This event brought together fighters from different martial arts backgrounds to compete under minimal rules, highlighting the strengths and weaknesses of various combat styles. The tournament was an early example of what would become the foundation of PRIDE's philosophy: showcasing diverse martial arts in an intense and competitive environment.

In 1997, Kingdom, another wrestling organization, emerged as a spiritual successor to UWFi. Kingdom aimed to continue the tradition of shoot wrestling while also experimenting with unscripted bouts. Though short-lived, Kingdom contributed to the growing popularity of realistic combat sports in Japan. These promotions collectively laid the groundwork for PRIDE FC's approach, combining the drama of professional wrestling with the authenticity of real fighting.

At the same time, kickboxing was experiencing a massive surge in popularity in Japan, thanks to the rise of K-1. Founded in 1993, K-1 organized high-energy tournaments that drew large crowds and television audiences. The promotion's emphasis on striking and action-packed bouts inspired PRIDE to adopt a similarly dynamic approach, focusing on exciting matchups and grand spectacles.

Together, these organizations and events shaped the combat sports landscape in Japan, creating an environment where PRIDE FC could thrive. The blending of martial arts, the emphasis on realism, and the demand for high-energy entertainment all contributed to PRIDE's eventual rise. By drawing inspiration from these predecessors, PRIDE built a promotion that would become one of the most influential in the history of MMA.

The Legacy of PRIDE FC

PRIDE FC may no longer exist, but its legacy is etched deeply into the history of mixed martial arts (MMA). The promotion stood out for its larger-than-life events, innovative rule set, and the unforgettable athletes who competed under its banner. It redefined combat sports, introducing fans to the idea that martial arts could be both a legitimate competition and an extraordinary spectacle. The echoes of PRIDE's influence can still be felt across the MMA world today.

One of PRIDE's most significant contributions was its ability to showcase the diversity of martial arts. By bringing together fighters from various disciplines such as Brazilian jiu-jitsu, wrestling, kickboxing, and sambo, PRIDE highlighted the strengths and weaknesses of each style. This diversity gave fans a broader understanding of martial arts and showcased the beauty of blending different techniques in combat. The unique matchups and "freak show" fights added another layer of excitement and unpredictability to every event.

PRIDE's rule set, which permitted soccer kicks, stomps, and knees to grounded opponents, was another aspect that set it apart. While these rules were controversial, they created an intense, fast-paced environment that appealed to fans who craved action. The 10-minute opening round was also unique, demanding incredible endurance and strategy from fighters. This format forced athletes to adapt, often leading to dramatic finishes and unforgettable moments.

The fighters themselves were a massive part of PRIDE's success. Legends like Fedor Emelianenko, Wanderlei Silva, and Mirko Cro Cop became household names due to their performances in the ring. These athletes not only displayed incredible skill but also embodied the warrior spirit that PRIDE sought to promote. Their battles remain some of the most iconic in MMA history, inspiring countless fighters who followed in their footsteps.

Beyond the competition, PRIDE's production value set a new standard for MMA promotions. Elaborate fighter entrances, dramatic opening ceremonies, and high-energy commentary turned each event into a spectacle. PRIDE treated its fighters like superstars and its events like major celebrations, creating an atmosphere that captivated fans. This focus on entertainment helped PRIDE build a global audience and cement its place in the history of combat sports.

The downfall of PRIDE, due to financial troubles and scandals, marked the end of an era, but it also paved the way for new opportunities. Fighters who made their names in PRIDE went on to compete in other promotions, most notably the UFC. Their success in these organizations carried the spirit of PRIDE forward, introducing its legacy to new audiences. The style, energy, and talent that defined PRIDE became a foundation upon which modern MMA was built.

Organizations like Rizin Fighting Federation, founded by PRIDE's co-creator Nobuyuki Sakakibara, have continued to honor its legacy. With similar production styles and a focus on exciting matchups, Rizin has kept PRIDE's philosophy alive in Japan. Other promotions worldwide have also drawn inspiration from PRIDE, adopting elements of its rule set, matchmaking approach, and production techniques.

The legacy of PRIDE is more than just its memorable fights and fighters. It is a testament to the power of innovation and the willingness to take risks in the pursuit of excellence. PRIDE showed the world what MMA could be: a sport that combines discipline and artistry with the thrill of competition. Its influence is a reminder of how one organization can change the trajectory of an entire industry.

As fans continue to look back on PRIDE with nostalgia, its place in MMA history remains secure. The promotion's unique blend of martial arts, entertainment, and passion will never be forgotten. For those who experienced the magic of PRIDE, it was more than just a fight organization—it was a celebration of the human spirit and the endless possibilities of combat sports.

Chapter 3: The Birth of PRIDE Fighting Championships

PRIDE Fighting Championships began in 1997 as an ambitious project to showcase a dream match between two legends from different worlds: Nobuhiko Takada, a popular Japanese pro wrestler, and Rickson Gracie, a celebrated Brazilian jiu-jitsu practitioner. Rickson had already gained fame in Japan by winning the 1994 and 1995 Vale Tudo Japan tournaments, cementing his reputation as one of the toughest fighters in the world. His brutal defeat of UWFi pro wrestler Yoji Anjo in a dojo storm at his Los Angeles gym further added to his mystique, making him a perfect opponent for Takada.

The inaugural event, held on October 11, 1997, took place at the iconic Tokyo Dome. Organized by KRS (Kakutougi Revolutionary Spirits), under the leadership of Hiromichi Momose, Naoto Morishita, and Nobuyuki Sakakibara, the event attracted an astonishing 47,000 fans. It wasn't just the fight fans who took notice—PRIDE's debut also gained significant attention from Japanese mass media, setting the stage for a new era in combat sports. This historic event marked the beginning of what would become a legendary MMA promotion.

The first PRIDE event was a spectacle. The Tokyo Dome was packed with energy, as fans eagerly awaited the clash between Takada and Gracie. Rickson's technical mastery of Brazilian jiu-jitsu was on full display, as he dominated Takada and secured a victory. While the result may have disappointed Takada's fans, the event's success was undeniable. PRIDE had proven that MMA could captivate a massive audience, and the demand for more events was clear.

Encouraged by this success, PRIDE promoters organized a rematch between Takada and Gracie in 1998. The second fight aimed to build on the momentum of the first event, attracting even more fans and media attention. Although Takada was unable to defeat Gracie, the event reinforced PRIDE's position as a serious player in the world of combat sports. The promotion's unique blend of martial arts and spectacle resonated with audiences, and plans for regular events were soon underway.

During its early years, PRIDE benefited from the growing popularity of K-1, a kickboxing promotion that had already captured the Japanese market. PRIDE capitalized on this by securing monthly broadcast slots on Fuji Television, as well as pay-per-view coverage on SKY PerfecTV, a newly launched satellite television channel. This extensive media exposure allowed PRIDE to reach millions of viewers, further solidifying its place in Japanese combat sports.

After its fourth event, PRIDE underwent a significant transformation. The promotion was taken over by Dream Stage Entertainment (DSE), a company formed by the former members of KRS. Under DSE's management, PRIDE was officially renamed PRIDE Fighting Championships. Naoto Morishita was appointed as its first chairman, and the organization began to evolve into the global powerhouse it would eventually become.

The early years of PRIDE were marked by rapid growth and bold experimentation. The promotion established itself as a unique blend of martial arts competition and high-energy entertainment. By featuring fighters from various backgrounds and promoting intense rivalries, PRIDE captured the imagination of fans around the world.

These formative years set the foundation for PRIDE's rise to prominence. With its roots in Japanese pro wrestling and its sights set on global expansion, PRIDE Fighting Championships emerged as a game-changing force in MMA. It combined the best elements of combat sports and entertainment, creating a legacy that continues to inspire fans and fighters alike.

The Enduring Legacy of PRIDE FC

PRIDE Fighting Championships left a lasting impact on the world of mixed martial arts. Even though the organization officially closed its doors in 2007, its influence continues to shape MMA. PRIDE was more than just a fight promotion; it was a cultural phenomenon that brought martial arts to life in a way no other organization had done before. Its legacy is celebrated by fighters and fans alike.

One of PRIDE's greatest contributions was its unique approach to MMA. It embraced the martial arts spirit, blending skill, discipline, and respect with the entertainment value of dramatic events. PRIDE didn't just host fights—it told stories. Each event was an experience, from the elaborate entrances to the thrilling matchups. This theatrical approach made PRIDE events unforgettable and elevated the sport to new heights.

The fighters who competed in PRIDE became legends in their own right. Athletes like Fedor Emelianenko, Wanderlei Silva, and Mirko Cro Cop built their legacies within the PRIDE ring. Their incredible performances inspired a generation of fighters and left fans with unforgettable memories. Even after PRIDE ended, these fighters carried its spirit into other organizations, ensuring its influence lived on.

PRIDE's innovative ruleset also played a role in its enduring appeal. The promotion allowed techniques like soccer kicks and stomps, which created a more aggressive and dynamic fighting style. While these rules were controversial, they added to the excitement of the matches and showcased the raw intensity of MMA. The 10-minute opening round tested fighters' endurance and strategy, setting PRIDE apart from other promotions.

The end of PRIDE marked a turning point for MMA. When the organization was purchased by Zuffa, the parent company of the UFC, many of PRIDE's top fighters transitioned to the UFC. This merger helped the UFC grow into the global powerhouse it is today, but it also marked the loss of PRIDE's distinct style and approach. For fans, it was bittersweet—the fighters lived on, but the unique atmosphere of PRIDE was gone.

Despite its closure, PRIDE's legacy is preserved in various ways. Organizations like Rizin Fighting Federation, founded by former PRIDE president Nobuyuki Sakakibara, aim to continue its tradition of spectacle and high-quality fights. Additionally, PRIDE's influence can be seen in the modern MMA landscape, where the blending of martial arts styles and the emphasis on entertainment remain central to the sport.

For those who experienced PRIDE firsthand, it remains a cherished memory. The thrill of watching iconic fights, the energy of the Japanese audience, and the larger-than-life atmosphere of PRIDE events are moments that cannot be replicated. Even for newer fans, PRIDE serves as a reminder of the rich history of MMA and the journey the sport has taken to reach its current popularity.

PRIDE FC was more than just a chapter in MMA history—it was a defining moment. It pushed the boundaries of what MMA could be and created a legacy that will be remembered for generations. While the organization may be gone, its spirit lives on in the hearts of fans and the fighters who continue to honor its memory.

Part Two: The Glory Years of PRIDE FC (2000–2006)

Chapter 4: The First Pride Grand Prix and Growing Global Fame

In 2000, PRIDE Fighting Championships launched its first-ever Grand Prix tournament. This openweight competition was designed to crown the "world's best fighter" and marked a pivotal moment in the promotion's history. The tournament spanned two major events, featuring sixteen fighters in the opening round. The victors advanced to the finals, held three months later, where they competed for the prestigious title.

The first round of the Grand Prix brought together a diverse lineup of fighters from across the globe, showcasing different styles and techniques. Fans were treated to intense battles, each fighter vying for a chance to advance to the finals. The tournament format added excitement, as viewers could follow their favorite fighters through multiple bouts, building anticipation for the climactic showdown.

The finals of the Grand Prix were held in May 2000 and represented a historic moment for PRIDE. It was the first time a PRIDE event was broadcast in the United States, opening the door to a new audience. American fighter Mark Coleman, known as "The Hammer," emerged as the tournament's champion. Coleman defeated Igor Vovchanchyn, a feared striker, in the final round, solidifying his legacy in MMA history.

PRIDE's expansion into the US market marked a turning point for the promotion. The broadcast of the Grand Prix finals introduced American fans to PRIDE's unique style of MMA, which included its distinctive rules and theatrical presentation. PRIDE's growing popularity in the US was further boosted by a highlights deal with Fox Sports Networks, which aired condensed versions of past events, and the release of DVDs featuring older PRIDE cards.

The DVDs became a key part of PRIDE's success in the United States. They allowed fans to experience the promotion's iconic fights and dramatic storytelling. PRIDE's international fanbase grew rapidly, as people around the world began to appreciate its combination of skillful martial arts and spectacle. This period marked the beginning of PRIDE's rise as a global MMA powerhouse.

English-language commentary played a significant role in connecting PRIDE with its new audience. Commentators like Stephen Quadros and Mauro Ranallo provided detailed play-by-play coverage, while analysts such as Bas Rutten and Frank Trigg added expert insights. Their enthusiasm and knowledge helped viewers understand the intricacies of the fights, making PRIDE events even more engaging.

The success of the 2000 Grand Prix laid the foundation for future tournaments and solidified PRIDE's reputation as a premier MMA organization. The openweight format allowed for dream matchups that transcended weight classes, creating a sense of unpredictability and excitement. PRIDE's tournaments became some of the most anticipated events in MMA, showcasing the best fighters from around the world.

By the early 2000s, PRIDE had firmly established itself as a dominant force in MMA. The Grand Prix tournaments, innovative production style, and a growing international fanbase set the promotion apart from its competitors. PRIDE's unique blend of martial arts and entertainment continued to captivate audiences, ensuring its place in the history of combat sports.

A Legacy Cemented by the 2000 Grand Prix

The 2000 PRIDE Grand Prix marked a turning point in the history of mixed martial arts and solidified PRIDE Fighting Championships as a global force. This tournament was not just a competition—it was a bold statement that PRIDE was ready to bring MMA to new heights. With its grand scale and global reach, the event laid a foundation that would resonate through the sport for years to come.

Mark Coleman's victory in the Grand Prix was a defining moment. Coleman, a former UFC champion and Olympic wrestler, showcased his grappling expertise and physical power throughout the tournament. His win against Igor Vovchanchyn in the final round was not only a personal triumph but also a testament to the effectiveness of his fighting style. Coleman became a symbol of PRIDE's mission to find and promote the best fighters in the world.

The tournament's broadcast in the United States was another groundbreaking achievement. For many American fans, this was their first introduction to PRIDE. The larger-than-life production, the intense fights, and the unique ruleset immediately captured their attention. PRIDE's appeal extended beyond traditional MMA fans, attracting those who appreciated the entertainment and drama the promotion offered.

The role of English-language commentary in expanding PRIDE's audience cannot be overstated. Commentators like Mauro Ranallo brought energy and excitement to every event, while analysts like Bas Rutten provided deep insights into the techniques and strategies on display. Together, they helped bridge the gap between PRIDE's Japanese roots and its growing international fanbase.

The success of the 2000 Grand Prix also highlighted the effectiveness of PRIDE's openweight format. Allowing fighters from different weight classes to compete created matchups that fans could only dream of seeing. This format celebrated the diversity of fighting styles and gave every fighter a chance to prove their worth on the biggest stage.

PRIDE's innovative approach to event production played a significant role in its rise. The combination of theatrical entrances, dramatic music, and high-stakes matchups made each event feel like a spectacle. This approach set PRIDE apart from other MMA promotions and kept fans eagerly awaiting each new card.

The aftermath of the 2000 Grand Prix saw PRIDE continue to grow in popularity. Its reputation as a premier MMA organization was now firmly established. The promotion attracted even more top-tier fighters and expanded its reach with new partnerships and broadcasting deals. PRIDE was no longer just a Japanese phenomenon—it was a global brand.

The legacy of the 2000 PRIDE Grand Prix endures as one of the most significant moments in MMA history. It showcased the best of what PRIDE had to offer:

world-class fighters, thrilling matchups, and a unique vision for the sport. For fans and fighters alike, this tournament remains a shining example of what made PRIDE Fighting Championships so special.

Chapter 5: Shockwave, Turmoil, and Leadership Changes

In August 2002, PRIDE teamed up with K-1, Japan's leading kickboxing promotion, to create one of the most ambitious events in combat sports history. The event, known as *Shockwave* or *PRIDE/K-1 Dynamite!!*, took place at the Tokyo National Stadium. It attracted over 71,000 fans, making it one of the largest fight events ever. The collaboration between PRIDE and K-1 brought together some of the best talent from both promotions, showcasing thrilling matchups that highlighted the diversity of combat sports.

Shockwave was a landmark event that symbolized the peak of PRIDE's popularity. The massive attendance and media coverage demonstrated the promotion's ability to captivate audiences on an unprecedented scale. The success of this event solidified PRIDE's reputation as a global leader in mixed martial arts and proved its appeal beyond MMA fans to a broader audience.

However, as PRIDE reached new heights, it also faced significant challenges. On January 13, 2003, DSE president Naoto Morishita was found dead in a hotel room. His death, ruled a suicide, shocked the MMA community and threw the organization into turmoil. Reports suggested personal issues as a possible factor, but the incident cast a shadow over PRIDE during a critical period in its growth.

The loss of Morishita left a leadership vacuum at Dream Stage Entertainment (DSE), PRIDE's parent company. Nobuyuki Sakakibara, who had been involved with PRIDE from the beginning, stepped into the role of president. His leadership style focused on stabilizing the organization and continuing its expansion, ensuring PRIDE remained on course despite the tragedy.

Sakakibara's tenure marked a period of both consolidation and innovation. He worked to strengthen PRIDE's relationships with fighters and promoters, ensuring that the promotion could continue to attract top talent. Former pro-wrestler Nobuhiko Takada also took on a more prominent role as general manager, bringing his experience and charisma to the forefront. Together, they sought to guide PRIDE through one of its most challenging periods.

Around this time, stories emerged about controversial practices within the organization. One such story involved Fedor Emelianenko, one of PRIDE's most dominant champions, reportedly being coerced at gunpoint to re-sign with the promotion. While such accounts added to the mystique of PRIDE, they also highlighted the complex and often shadowy dynamics behind the scenes.

Despite the turmoil, PRIDE continued to produce high-quality events and maintain its position as a premier MMA organization. The promotion's ability to deliver captivating fights and showcase elite fighters kept fans engaged and loyal. PRIDE's events were not just about the competition but also about the spectacle, with dramatic entrances, intense rivalries, and high-stakes matchups.

By the mid-2000s, PRIDE had weathered significant challenges and continued to thrive. Events like

Shockwave proved the promotion's ability to achieve extraordinary success, while the leadership changes and controversies highlighted its resilience in the face of adversity. PRIDE's journey during this time was a testament to its enduring appeal and its role as a trailblazer in the world of mixed martial arts.

Overcoming Chaos to Solidify PRIDE's Place in MMA History

The events between 2002 and 2003 marked a pivotal moment for PRIDE Fighting Championships. The *Shockwave* collaboration with K-1 was a high point, showcasing PRIDE's ability to create large-scale spectacles that captured global attention. With over 71,000 fans attending, the event reinforced PRIDE's position as a leader in combat sports and demonstrated how MMA could transcend its niche audience to appeal to the masses. This event set a new benchmark for MMA promotions worldwide.

Despite this success, the sudden death of Naoto Morishita in January 2003 cast a shadow over the organization. The tragedy threatened to derail the momentum PRIDE had built, especially given Morishita's instrumental role in guiding the promotion. His passing was a stark reminder of the intense pressures behind the scenes, even as PRIDE flourished on the global stage.

Nobuyuki Sakakibara's rise to leadership was a critical turning point. His steady hand and vision for the promotion helped stabilize PRIDE during an uncertain time. Alongside general manager Nobuhiko Takada, Sakakibara worked to ensure that PRIDE remained a dominant force in MMA. Together, they navigated challenges and maintained the promotion's reputation for delivering exciting, high-quality events.

The controversies surrounding this era only added to PRIDE's mystique. Stories about coercion, including the alleged incident involving Fedor Emelianenko, highlighted the complex and sometimes murky operations behind the scenes. While these accounts tarnished PRIDE's image in some circles, they also contributed to its aura as a promotion willing to go to great lengths to secure its position at the top.

PRIDE's ability to continue growing despite these internal struggles was a testament to its strong foundation. Its unique blend of theatricality and elite-level competition resonated with fans around the world. Events were not just sporting contests—they were cultural phenomena, filled with drama, spectacle, and larger-than-life personalities.

By navigating both triumph and turmoil, PRIDE showcased its resilience. The leadership transition demonstrated that the organization could adapt to challenges while staying true to its core mission of providing world-class MMA events. Fans continued to support PRIDE because of its ability to deliver unforgettable moments and showcase the best fighters from around the globe.

The legacy of this chapter lies in PRIDE's determination to overcome adversity while setting new standards for MMA promotions. The partnership with K-1 and the *Shockwave* event proved that collaboration could create something extraordinary, while the struggles behind the scenes highlighted the complexities of running a groundbreaking promotion.

As PRIDE moved forward, it carried with it the lessons of this turbulent time. The combination of visionary leadership, passionate fans, and a roster of talented fighters ensured that PRIDE would remain a cornerstone of MMA history, even as it continued to evolve in the years ahead.

Chapter 6: The Launch of PRIDE Bushido and the Rise of Lighter Weight Classes

In 2003, PRIDE Fighting Championships launched the Bushido series, a groundbreaking addition to its roster of events. The Bushido series aimed to spotlight lighter weight classes, primarily focusing on lightweights and welterweights. This shift allowed PRIDE to highlight fighters who were often overshadowed by the heavyweights dominating the main PRIDE events. By emphasizing speed, technique, and action, Bushido brought a fresh and dynamic approach to MMA.

The Bushido events introduced a new fight format designed to create a faster-paced experience for fans. Unlike regular PRIDE matches, Bushido bouts consisted of one ten-minute round followed by one five-minute round. This shortened format encouraged fighters to adopt aggressive strategies, knowing they had less time to secure a win. The faster pace and high energy of these matches quickly became a signature of the Bushido series.

One of the most innovative elements of Bushido was the introduction of the "yellow card" system. If a fighter was deemed to be stalling or avoiding action, the referee could issue a yellow card, which not only served as a warning but also resulted in a deduction from the fighter's purse. This system was designed to discourage inactivity and ensure that matches remained exciting for fans. The yellow card became a defining feature of Bushido, reinforcing PRIDE's commitment to delivering action-packed fights.

The focus on lighter weight classes in Bushido allowed fighters with speed and technical prowess to shine. Athletes in the lightweight and welterweight divisions brought a different style of competition, showcasing fast-paced striking, fluid grappling, and relentless energy. Fighters like Takanori Gomi and Hayato "Mach" Sakurai emerged as stars of the series, captivating audiences with their skills and dynamic performances.

Bushido also became a platform for international talent. By bringing in fighters from around the world, PRIDE expanded its reach and introduced fans to a diverse array of fighting styles. The inclusion of athletes from different countries added to the appeal of Bushido, creating matchups that were both unpredictable and thrilling. This global approach further cemented PRIDE's reputation as a premier MMA organization.

The Bushido events didn't just focus on competition— they also maintained the theatrical elements that PRIDE was known for. From elaborate entrances to dramatic matchups, the series retained the larger-than-life atmosphere that fans had come to expect from PRIDE. This combination of fast-paced action and entertainment made Bushido a fan favorite and a critical part of PRIDE's growth.

While the Bushido series primarily showcased lighter weight classes, it wasn't exclusive to them. Occasionally, fighters from heavier divisions participated, adding variety to the events. This inclusivity ensured that Bushido appealed to a broad audience while staying true to its mission of promoting lighter weight fighters.

The success of the Bushido series demonstrated PRIDE's ability to innovate and adapt. By creating a platform for lighter weight fighters and emphasizing action over stalling, Bushido brought a new dimension to PRIDE's events. The series became an integral part of PRIDE's legacy, showing that the organization was not only about grand spectacles but also about evolving the sport and providing opportunities for all fighters to shine.

The Legacy of PRIDE Bushido

The PRIDE Bushido series left an indelible mark on the world of mixed martial arts. By focusing on lighter weight classes and faster-paced bouts, Bushido filled a niche that had been largely overlooked in mainstream MMA. It gave fighters like Takanori Gomi, Joachim Hansen, and others a platform to showcase their unique talents, setting the stage for some of the most thrilling matchups in PRIDE's history.

The introduction of innovative elements like the "yellow card" system further distinguished Bushido from other MMA promotions. By penalizing inactivity and rewarding aggression, this rule emphasized action, keeping the audience on the edge of their seats. Fans appreciated the urgency it brought to matches, creating an atmosphere of constant excitement and unpredictability.

Bushido also exemplified PRIDE's commitment to global MMA by featuring fighters from various countries. This international approach not only diversified the roster but also expanded the sport's appeal worldwide. Fighters from Japan, Brazil, the United States, and beyond came together under the

Bushido banner, embodying the spirit of true martial arts competition.

The series stood as a testament to PRIDE's adaptability and forward-thinking approach. While the organization was renowned for its heavyweight and open-weight spectacles, Bushido proved that lighter weight fighters could deliver equally compelling performances. This focus helped to grow the popularity of weight classes like lightweight and welterweight, paving the way for their prominence in modern MMA.

Bushido's influence extended beyond its matches. It reshaped perceptions of what MMA could be, showing that smaller fighters with technical precision and high-energy styles were just as capable of drawing crowds as their heavier counterparts. This shift in focus helped to redefine the sport, influencing promotions that followed.

Despite its relatively short run, Bushido left a lasting legacy. Its innovative format, emphasis on action, and celebration of lighter weight classes set a new standard in MMA. While PRIDE itself eventually came to an end, the spirit of Bushido lived on in other promotions and in the hearts of fans who witnessed its thrilling events.

Bushido also highlighted the value of innovation in sports. By challenging conventions and experimenting with new ideas, PRIDE demonstrated that progress in MMA wasn't just about the fighters—it was also about the structure and presentation of events. The series became a model for how to push the boundaries of what MMA could offer.

In the grand story of PRIDE Fighting Championships, Bushido represents a vital chapter. It showcased the organization's ability to evolve, innovate, and bring something fresh to the world of combat sports. While PRIDE as a whole is remembered for its grandeur and spectacle, Bushido stands out as a symbol of the promotion's dedication to the sport itself—a commitment to action, diversity, and the relentless pursuit of excellence.

Chapter 7: The Return of the Grand Prix Format

In 2003, PRIDE Fighting Championships revived its popular Grand Prix tournament format, thrilling fans with a series of events focused on middleweight fighters. The tournament began with *PRIDE Total Elimination 2003*, which set the stage for an intense competition. Sixteen fighters competed in the opening round, showcasing their skills in dramatic and hard-fought battles. The winners advanced to *Final Conflict 2003*, where the tournament concluded with a thrilling display of martial arts mastery.

The Grand Prix format added a layer of excitement and unpredictability to PRIDE events. Fans eagerly anticipated seeing their favorite fighters tested in a tournament setting, where endurance and strategy were as crucial as raw talent. The middleweight Grand Prix of 2003 brought together top competitors like Wanderlei Silva and Quinton "Rampage" Jackson, both of whom became icons of the sport through their performances in this tournament.

Building on the success of 2003, PRIDE expanded its Grand Prix format in 2004. The tournament now included three stages, starting with *Total Elimination*, followed by *Critical Countdown*, and culminating in *Final Conflict*. This extended format allowed fighters to demonstrate their skills over multiple rounds, adding more drama and depth to the competition. The 2004 heavyweight Grand Prix featured some of the most legendary names in MMA, including Fedor Emelianenko and Antonio Rodrigo Nogueira, whose rivalry captivated fans worldwide.

The annual Grand Prix tournaments became a defining feature of PRIDE. Each year brought a new theme and fresh matchups, keeping fans engaged and eager for more. In 2005, the middleweight Grand Prix returned, featuring iconic moments such as Wanderlei Silva's battles and Mauricio "Shogun" Rua's rise to prominence. The format continued to attract top talent, showcasing fighters from different countries and martial arts backgrounds.

PRIDE took things to another level in 2006 with the introduction of the openweight Grand Prix. This tournament removed weight class restrictions, allowing fighters of all sizes to compete against one another. The openweight format created unique and memorable matchups, such as lighter fighters taking on much larger opponents. Mirko Cro Cop Filipović, known for his devastating head kicks, emerged as the winner, cementing his legacy in PRIDE history.

The Grand Prix tournaments also played a significant role in PRIDE's global popularity. The format was easy for fans to understand, even if they were new to MMA, and it provided a clear narrative for each year's events. The drama of elimination rounds and the prestige of winning a Grand Prix title drew in viewers from around the world, further solidifying PRIDE's reputation as a premier MMA organization.

These tournaments were not without challenges. The grueling nature of fighting multiple times in a short period tested fighters physically and mentally. However, this difficulty also made victories even more impressive, as champions needed to demonstrate exceptional skill, endurance, and adaptability to succeed.

By 2006, PRIDE's Grand Prix tournaments had become legendary, leaving a lasting impact on the world of MMA. They showcased the best fighters of their time, created unforgettable moments, and elevated the sport to new heights. The Grand Prix format remains a beloved part of PRIDE's legacy, celebrated by fans and fighters alike for its ability to deliver excitement, drama, and unparalleled competition.

The Legacy of PRIDE's Grand Prix Tournaments

The PRIDE Grand Prix tournaments remain one of the most iconic chapters in mixed martial arts history, capturing the spirit of competition and the artistry of combat. These tournaments brought fighters from different disciplines, backgrounds, and countries into the spotlight, creating a stage where legends were born. From the middleweight battles of 2003 to the openweight extravaganza of 2006, these tournaments solidified PRIDE's reputation as a groundbreaking MMA organization.

What made the Grand Prix format so special was its emphasis on showcasing a fighter's endurance, strategy, and versatility. Winning a tournament required not only raw skill but also the ability to adapt to different opponents and overcome physical fatigue. The champions of these events, such as Fedor Emelianenko and Mirko Cro Cop, became symbols of resilience and mastery in the sport. Their victories resonated far beyond Japan, inspiring fans around the globe.

The tournaments also demonstrated PRIDE's commitment to creating an unparalleled spectacle.

Each event was meticulously produced, with grand entrances, roaring crowds, and a sense of drama that made every fight feel like a pivotal moment. This theatrical flair elevated the tournaments, making them as much about the experience as the competition.

The openweight Grand Prix of 2006, in particular, epitomized the unpredictability and excitement that PRIDE was known for. By removing weight class restrictions, the tournament opened the door to unique matchups that would not have been possible elsewhere. It challenged fighters to go beyond their limits and pushed the boundaries of what was considered possible in MMA.

The success of these tournaments also helped PRIDE expand its influence internationally. Through television deals, DVD releases, and the fervent passion of its fanbase, PRIDE brought its tournaments to audiences far beyond Japan. Fighters who shone in the Grand Prix events gained global recognition, often going on to influence MMA culture and style in other organizations.

However, the tournaments were not without controversy. The grueling nature of competing multiple times in a short span raised questions about fighter safety and the long-term effects on their health. Despite these challenges, the tournaments' legacy is overwhelmingly positive, remembered for the incredible feats of athleticism and the unforgettable moments they produced.

Looking back, the PRIDE Grand Prix tournaments stand as a testament to the creativity and ambition of the organization. They were a perfect blend of martial arts tradition and innovation, paying homage to the past while pushing the sport forward. These events left a lasting impact, not only on the fighters who participated but also on the fans who watched in awe.

As we reflect on this era, the Grand Prix tournaments remind us of the magic that happens when skill, determination, and showmanship come together. They are a cherished part of PRIDE's history, a time when the sport reached new heights and brought people together to celebrate the universal language of combat.

Part Three: The Fall of PRIDE: From Glory to Uncertainty

Chapter 8: Collaboration and Conflict (2006)

In 2006, PRIDE's parent company, Dream Stage Entertainment (DSE), announced plans to collaborate with North America's Ultimate Fighting Championship (UFC). This partnership aimed to bring PRIDE's top fighters to a wider audience and merge the best talent from both organizations. The announcement included an exciting prospect: a match between PRIDE's superstar Wanderlei Silva and the UFC's Chuck Liddell. Fans around the world were thrilled by the possibility of this dream fight, as it promised to unite two dominant MMA promotions.

Despite the initial buzz, tensions quickly surfaced. UFC President Dana White publicly criticized the Japanese promoters, citing difficulties in negotiations. The cultural and operational differences between the organizations made collaboration challenging. White's comment that "the Japanese are very hard to do business with" highlighted these struggles. The planned Silva vs. Liddell bout was canceled, leaving fans disappointed and skeptical about future collaborations.

The history between PRIDE and UFC already had its share of complications. Back in 2003, UFC had sent Chuck Liddell to compete in PRIDE's Middleweight Grand Prix. The expectation was that Liddell would progress through the tournament to face Wanderlei Silva in the finals. However, those plans fell apart when Liddell was defeated in the semi-finals by Quinton "Rampage" Jackson. Jackson went on to fight Silva in the finals, where he suffered a devastating loss.

This series of events deepened the competitive rivalry between PRIDE and the UFC. Both organizations aimed to establish themselves as the premier MMA promotion in the world. While PRIDE's production value, ruleset, and international roster drew global attention, the UFC's growing American fanbase and stronghold in the North American market gave it an edge.

Behind the scenes, PRIDE was also dealing with internal challenges. The loss of key broadcasting deals in Japan, partly due to scandals, had weakened the organization financially. PRIDE's reliance on pay-per-view and international DVD sales was not enough to sustain its ambitious operations. The strain was visible as DSE scrambled to find new ways to keep the organization afloat.

The failure of the Liddell-Silva match was symbolic of PRIDE's struggles during this period. It represented the broader difficulties of merging two vastly different MMA cultures and business models. Fans continued to clamor for a unified MMA platform, but the political and logistical hurdles proved too great.

Despite these setbacks, PRIDE remained determined to showcase its talent on a global stage. The organization continued to promote events featuring its iconic fighters, maintaining its reputation as the home of some of the most thrilling bouts in MMA history. However, the cracks in its foundation were becoming increasingly evident, and its ability to compete with the UFC was waning.

The year 2006 marked a turning point for PRIDE. While its fighters remained among the best in the world, the organization's future was clouded by uncertainty. The dream of a fully unified MMA landscape seemed further away than ever, leaving fans to wonder what lay ahead for the once-dominant PRIDE Fighting Championships.

The Struggles of Collaboration and PRIDE's Decline

The events of 2006 underscored the challenges PRIDE faced as it attempted to bridge the gap between Japanese and North American MMA. The year began with great promise, as PRIDE sought to integrate its fighters with the UFC. This bold move was meant to showcase PRIDE's stars like Wanderlei Silva to a global audience. However, the inability to execute the highly anticipated Silva vs. Chuck Liddell fight became a symbol of the difficulties in uniting two contrasting MMA worlds.

The collaboration was fraught with cultural and operational misunderstandings. PRIDE's flashy presentation and focus on Japanese traditions contrasted sharply with the UFC's business-oriented, North American style. Dana White's frustration with negotiations highlighted how challenging it was to align the goals of these two powerhouse promotions. The failure of this partnership disappointed fans who hoped to see the best fighters from both organizations face off.

While PRIDE tried to maintain its image as a global leader in MMA, the cracks in its foundation were growing. The organization was losing its grip on the Japanese market due to scandals that alienated key broadcasters. This loss of media coverage significantly reduced its revenue, forcing PRIDE to rely more on international audiences. However, these efforts couldn't make up for the setbacks at home.

PRIDE's internal challenges were amplified by external competition. The UFC's rising dominance in North America put additional pressure on PRIDE to stay relevant. As the UFC expanded its roster and gained more international recognition, PRIDE struggled to keep pace, despite having many of the world's best fighters.

The disappointment surrounding the failed Liddell-Silva bout was emblematic of a larger issue: PRIDE's inability to adapt to the rapidly changing MMA landscape. The organization was built on a foundation of innovation and spectacle, but the challenges of maintaining its status as a global leader became too great.

Despite these challenges, PRIDE continued to deliver memorable events and showcased legendary fighters. The organization's dedication to its unique identity ensured that it remained a favorite among hardcore MMA fans. Yet, the financial and operational struggles made it clear that PRIDE's dominance was slipping.

The year 2006 marked the beginning of the end for PRIDE as it faced increasing difficulties in competing with the UFC. While PRIDE's fighters and fans remained loyal, the organization's future looked uncertain. The inability to bridge the cultural and business gaps with the UFC highlighted the challenges of globalizing MMA.

PRIDE's decline was a bittersweet chapter in MMA history. It remained a symbol of innovation and excitement, but its struggles served as a reminder of the complexities of sustaining success in the fast-evolving world of combat sports. The chapter closed with a sense of nostalgia for what PRIDE had achieved and a hint of sadness for what it could no longer sustain.

Chapter 9: Pride's Expansion to the United States

Pride Fighting Championships reached a milestone in 2006 by hosting its first-ever MMA event outside Japan. Pride 32: The Real Deal was held on October 21, 2006, at the Thomas & Mack Center in Paradise, Nevada. The event marked an important step in Pride's efforts to expand into the North American market. Drawing an audience of 11,727 fans, the show demonstrated the growing global appeal of Pride and its roster of elite fighters.

This event had a unique atmosphere. For the first time, Pride adapted to Nevada's athletic commission rules, including stricter regulations on certain moves like soccer kicks and stomps, which were staples of Pride events in Japan. Despite these adjustments, the fights retained the explosive energy and spectacle fans had come to expect. Fighters such as Wanderlei Silva, Fedor Emelianenko, and Josh Barnett became household names among MMA enthusiasts in the United States.

The Real Deal featured several highly anticipated bouts, showcasing both established Pride stars and a few American fighters. These matchups provided U.S. audiences with a taste of Pride's action-packed events and its dramatic entrances, intense rivalries, and world-class production values. This event underscored Pride's commitment to delivering high-quality MMA entertainment on a global stage.

While the Nevada debut was a success in many ways, it also highlighted the challenges Pride faced in expanding beyond its home base in Japan. Operating in a new market meant navigating different regulations, building relationships with American broadcasters, and competing directly with the UFC, which was already well-established in North America. Despite these obstacles, the Nevada event proved that Pride had a dedicated fanbase outside Japan.

Pride's expansion into the U.S. also had a profound impact on fighters. Many athletes saw the event as an opportunity to gain greater international exposure. Competing in the United States opened doors for some to eventually transition to other promotions, including the UFC, further boosting their careers. For Pride, this was a step toward bridging the gap between Japanese and American MMA markets.

However, the financial and logistical pressures of holding events overseas began to strain Pride's resources. While the Nevada event was celebrated for its strong attendance and production, the costs of organizing shows outside Japan, coupled with the ongoing competition with the UFC, presented significant challenges. These pressures hinted at the struggles that would soon affect the organization.

Despite these challenges, Pride continued to maintain its reputation as a premier MMA organization. The success of Pride 32 inspired hope that more U.S. events would follow, bringing the brand to even wider audiences. For many fans, the event symbolized the peak of Pride's ambitions and its ability to compete on a global level.

The Nevada debut represented a turning point for Pride Fighting Championships. It was both a testament to its growth and a reminder of the complexities of international expansion. While Pride's dominance in Japan remained strong, the push to establish a foothold in the United States revealed the organization's vision for a truly global MMA stage.

Pride's U.S. Debut and Its Global Legacy

The success of Pride 32: The Real Deal was a defining moment for Pride Fighting Championships, marking the promotion's first step into the global MMA arena. This event brought Pride's unique style and presentation to a new audience, offering a glimpse into the grandeur and intensity that had captivated Japanese fans for years. It proved that Pride had the potential to thrive internationally, setting a high standard for MMA events outside its home country.

The decision to host an event in Nevada showcased Pride's ambition to compete on a global stage. The transition from Japan to the U.S. was not without challenges, but it highlighted the organization's commitment to growing its brand and reaching new fans. By adhering to Nevada's strict athletic commission rules, Pride demonstrated its adaptability while maintaining the essence of its events, including high-energy fights and dramatic showmanship.

For fighters, the U.S. debut was more than just a competition; it was an opportunity to gain exposure in a lucrative and growing MMA market. Fighters like Wanderlei Silva and Josh Barnett captured the imagination of U.S. audiences, solidifying their places as international MMA stars. These athletes represented the best of Pride and helped bridge the gap between Japanese and American MMA styles.

Despite the initial success of Pride 32, the event also underscored the challenges of expanding into a new market. Competing directly with the UFC in its home territory meant facing a well-established rival with deep local roots. While Pride brought a distinct flavor to MMA, building a sustainable presence in the U.S. required significant financial and logistical investment, which strained the organization's resources.

The debut in Nevada highlighted the contrasting philosophies of Pride and the UFC. Pride's focus on spectacle, storytelling, and elaborate production set it apart from the more straightforward approach of its American counterpart. This difference appealed to many fans, but it also revealed the difficulty of blending the two cultures of MMA while retaining each organization's identity.

Although Pride 32 did not immediately lead to a long-term U.S. expansion, it served as a milestone in the history of MMA. The event's success demonstrated the universal appeal of the sport and the potential for promotions to grow beyond their traditional markets. For fans, it offered a chance to experience the best of Pride and enjoy matchups that showcased the skill and diversity of its fighters.

The Nevada event remains a significant chapter in Pride's story. It symbolized both the heights the organization could achieve and the obstacles it faced in pursuing its global vision. As Pride continued to hold events in Japan, the lessons learned from Pride 32 shaped its approach to international growth, even as it navigated financial and competitive pressures.

In retrospect, Pride 32 was more than just an event— it was a moment of ambition and innovation in the world of MMA. It left an indelible mark on the sport, inspiring future promotions to think globally and reminding fans of the unique qualities that made Pride a legend in the history of mixed martial arts.

Chapter 10: The End of Pride's Golden Era

In June 2006, Fuji Network, one of Japan's major broadcasters, terminated its contract with Pride Fighting Championships due to a breach of agreement by Dream Stage Entertainment (DSE), Pride's parent company. The abrupt decision shocked the MMA world and marked the beginning of significant challenges for Pride. Losing Fuji TV's massive platform meant a steep decline in exposure and revenue for the organization, jeopardizing its position as a top MMA promotion.

The loss of the Fuji deal left Pride with only SKY PerfecTV, a pay-per-view outlet in Japan. Although dedicated fans continued to support Pride through this medium, the financial blow was substantial. The revenue from network television had been a critical part of Pride's business model, funding its lavish productions and international expansion. Without it, Pride faced an uphill battle to maintain its operations at the same scale.

Speculation swirled in the Japanese media about the reasons behind Fuji's decision. Reports, particularly from the tabloid *Shukan Gendai*, alleged that DSE had ties to the infamous yakuza crime syndicate. These allegations damaged Pride's reputation and created a cloud of mistrust around the organization. While DSE denied any wrongdoing, the rumors persisted, further complicating its efforts to secure new business partnerships.

Despite these challenges, DSE vowed to continue with Pride's ambitious plans. In February 2007, Pride held its second U.S. event, Pride 33: Second Coming, in Las Vegas. The event featured thrilling fights and demonstrated the organization's commitment to expanding internationally. However, the financial strain of losing its Japanese television deal loomed over these efforts, casting doubt on Pride's long-term viability.

The Las Vegas event highlighted Pride's enduring appeal among MMA fans. Fighters like Dan Henderson, Wanderlei Silva, and Mauricio "Shogun" Rua delivered memorable performances, showcasing the high level of talent that had defined Pride's roster. The event attracted attention from both fans and competitors in the U.S., further solidifying Pride's legacy as a premier MMA promotion.

Behind the scenes, however, the organization's financial difficulties were mounting. The costs of hosting large-scale events, coupled with declining revenue, created a precarious situation for DSE. Efforts to find new investors or media partners proved challenging, especially with the ongoing speculation about yakuza connections. Pride's management faced an increasingly complex landscape as they sought to stabilize the organization.

As the challenges grew, comparisons between Pride and its American counterpart, the Ultimate Fighting Championship (UFC), became more frequent. The UFC, bolstered by its success in the U.S. and a steady stream of pay-per-view income, appeared to be in a stronger position to dominate the global MMA market. This dynamic added pressure on Pride to innovate and adapt, even as its resources dwindled.

The termination of the Fuji TV contract marked a turning point in Pride's history. It signaled the end of its golden era and set the stage for its eventual decline. Despite the obstacles, Pride's legacy endured, thanks to its unforgettable events, world-class fighters, and the passion of its fans. The organization's story serves as a testament to the highs and lows of MMA, reflecting both the potential and the challenges of building a global sports phenomenon.

Pride's Struggles in 2006-2007: A Turning Point

The aftermath of losing the Fuji TV contract marked a significant decline for Pride Fighting Championships, yet it also revealed the organization's determination to persevere. The loss of network television exposure was a devastating blow, but Pride's resilience during this period demonstrated its commitment to delivering high-quality events despite mounting challenges.

Pride 33: Second Coming in Las Vegas was a critical moment during this tumultuous time. Despite financial struggles, the event showcased Pride's ability to organize thrilling fights and maintain its reputation as a world-class MMA promotion. The fighters gave their all, and the event captured the attention of fans worldwide, proving that Pride's spirit remained strong even under immense pressure.

However, the financial instability caused by losing the lucrative Fuji TV deal could not be ignored. The rumors of yakuza connections, whether true or not, had already tarnished the organization's reputation. This made it difficult to find new sponsors or media partners willing to associate themselves with Pride, further exacerbating its financial difficulties.

The efforts to expand internationally, including hosting events in the United States, highlighted Pride's ambitious vision. Yet, the costs of operating on a global scale without sufficient revenue from its home market in Japan were unsustainable. These challenges put immense strain on DSE, as they struggled to keep the organization afloat while maintaining the high production values that fans had come to expect.

Despite these issues, Pride's legacy as a pioneer in MMA remained intact. The organization continued to attract top talent and deliver memorable bouts that would go down in history. Fighters like Fedor Emelianenko, Wanderlei Silva, and others played a crucial role in keeping fans engaged and reinforcing Pride's reputation as a premier MMA promotion.

The UFC's growing dominance during this period added another layer of difficulty for Pride. As the UFC expanded its reach and gained traction in the global MMA market, Pride's struggles became more pronounced. The rivalry between the two organizations was a defining aspect of this era, with fans often debating the merits of each promotion and its fighters.

The termination of the Fuji TV deal was not just a setback for Pride; it was a defining moment that forced the organization to confront its vulnerabilities. The loss of revenue and reputation created a challenging environment that tested the resolve of everyone involved with Pride. Yet, even in the face of adversity, Pride managed to leave a lasting impact on the MMA world.

Ultimately, this chapter in Pride's history serves as a reminder of the challenges faced by even the most successful organizations. It highlights the importance of resilience, innovation, and adaptability in the face of adversity. While Pride's decline was inevitable given the circumstances, its contributions to the sport of MMA continue to be celebrated by fans and fighters alike.

Chapter 11: The Tyson Dream That Never Came True

In late 2006, the prospect of Mike Tyson fighting in Pride Fighting Championships sparked excitement and controversy. DSE, Pride's parent company, hinted at plans to feature Tyson in a unique match during its annual New Year's Eve event. The idea was to pit the former boxing world champion against a Pride fighter under boxing rules, creating a spectacle that would attract global attention. This proposal was bold, blending Tyson's star power with Pride's reputation for dramatic and unpredictable events.

However, there were immediate hurdles to overcome. Tyson's criminal record prohibited him from entering Japan, making it impossible to hold the fight on Japanese soil. To address this issue, Pride considered alternative venues, with Macau, China, emerging as a potential host. The plan included broadcasting the fight live on large screens at the Saitama Super Arena, where the rest of the New Year's Eve MMA card would be held. This setup was meant to maintain the event's connection to its Japanese audience while accommodating Tyson's legal restrictions.

The idea of Tyson competing under boxing rules against a Pride fighter was intriguing but posed significant logistical and legal challenges. Boxing and MMA operate under different regulatory frameworks, and the proposed fight would have required special arrangements to ensure compliance with various athletic commissions. Additionally, questions arose about who Tyson's opponent would be, as few MMA fighters would have been prepared to face him under boxing rules.

Despite these challenges, the possibility of Tyson's involvement generated immense media buzz. Tyson was one of the most recognizable names in combat sports, and his inclusion would have elevated Pride's profile internationally. Fans speculated about potential matchups and debated the implications of a boxing match within the context of an MMA event.

Ultimately, the fight did not materialize. The reasons were likely a combination of logistical difficulties, regulatory obstacles, and financial considerations. Organizing such a high-profile event in a foreign country would have required significant resources, and the return on investment was uncertain. Additionally, Tyson's personal and legal troubles may have further complicated negotiations, making the proposed fight untenable.

The absence of the Tyson fight was a missed opportunity for Pride, especially as the organization faced mounting challenges in 2006 and 2007. The potential crossover appeal of featuring a boxing icon in an MMA event could have introduced new fans to Pride and boosted its international reputation. However, the ambitious nature of the proposal underscored Pride's willingness to think outside the box and push the boundaries of traditional combat sports.

Despite the disappointment of the canceled Tyson bout, Pride's New Year's Eve show went on as planned. The event featured a series of memorable MMA fights that showcased the skill and determination of Pride's roster. While the Tyson dream remained unfulfilled, the organization continued to deliver exciting and innovative events that resonated with its fanbase.

In retrospect, the idea of bringing Mike Tyson to Pride was emblematic of the organization's creative and daring approach to promotion. It highlighted Pride's ambition to transcend the traditional boundaries of MMA and create events that were as much about spectacle as sport. Although the fight never happened, the story of Tyson's proposed involvement remains a fascinating chapter in Pride's history.

Tyson's Absence and Pride's Unyielding Ambition

The story of Mike Tyson's proposed appearance in Pride Fighting Championships is one of both ambition and disappointment. The idea of integrating Tyson's legendary boxing reputation into Pride's MMA framework reflected the organization's bold approach to entertainment and combat sports. The proposed fight, however, became an unrealized dream, leaving fans to wonder what might have been.

For Pride, Tyson represented more than just a famous name. He symbolized a bridge between two worlds: traditional boxing and the rising popularity of mixed martial arts. A Tyson fight under Pride's banner could have brought new fans, media attention, and perhaps a surge in global popularity. Yet, the hurdles to making it happen—Tyson's criminal record barring his entry into Japan and the logistical challenges of hosting the fight in Macau—proved insurmountable.

The cancellation of the Tyson bout did not diminish the creative spirit that defined Pride. Instead, it highlighted the lengths to which the organization would go to captivate its audience. By envisioning such an event, Pride reinforced its identity as a promotion willing to take risks and think beyond the conventional boundaries of MMA.

While Tyson's fight never took place, Pride's New Year's Eve show still delivered excitement and action. The MMA bouts showcased the talent and diversity of its fighters, affirming Pride's commitment to providing world-class competition. Even without Tyson, the event demonstrated that Pride could stand on its own as a premier MMA organization.

In the context of Pride's history, the Tyson story remains a fascinating "what-if" moment. It reflects both the organization's strengths—its ambition, creativity, and willingness to innovate—and its challenges, including navigating complex legal and logistical issues. It is a reminder of how Pride continuously sought to push the envelope, even if not every idea came to fruition.

For fans, the proposed Tyson fight is a lingering mystery. What kind of spectacle would it have been? Would it have succeeded in merging the audiences of boxing and MMA? Or would it have created a spectacle overshadowing the sport itself? These unanswered questions add an air of intrigue to Pride's legacy.

As Pride continued to face challenges in the following years, the missed Tyson opportunity became emblematic of the organization's larger struggles. While Pride's vision and ambition were unparalleled, it operated in an environment that was often unforgiving of its grand ideas. The Tyson saga underscores the highs and lows that defined Pride's journey as a trailblazer in MMA history.

Ultimately, Tyson's absence was not a failure but a testament to Pride's enduring belief in the extraordinary. It dared to dream big and left an indelible mark on the world of combat sports, even in its unfulfilled aspirations. This spirit of ambition, even when unmet, is what continues to make Pride Fighting Championships a legend in the history of MMA.

Chapter 12 : The End of Bushido and a New Direction for Pride

In late 2006, Pride announced significant changes to its event structure, including the discontinuation of the Bushido series. These events, which focused on lighter weight classes and fast-paced fights, had gained a loyal following. Integrating these matches into regular Pride events aimed to consolidate the promotion's offerings and bring more attention to all fighters, regardless of weight class. This decision marked the end of an era for Bushido, but it also symbolized a shift toward unifying Pride's brand under a single, cohesive event style.

Pride's vision for the future included a new system for Grand Prix tournaments. Instead of holding multiple tournaments across weight classes annually, the organization planned a four-year cycle, with each year dedicated to one specific weight class. This strategy was intended to build anticipation and excitement around each Grand Prix, making them even more prestigious. The first Grand Prix in this cycle was supposed to focus on the lightweight division. Unfortunately, this tournament never materialized, leaving fans disappointed and questioning Pride's ability to execute its ambitious plans.

The cancellation of the lightweight Grand Prix was a significant setback. Pride had promised a showcase for its talented lighter-weight fighters, but logistical challenges and financial pressures likely contributed to the decision to scrap the tournament. This missed opportunity highlighted the difficulties Pride faced as it attempted to innovate while maintaining its high production standards and international appeal.

Despite these challenges, Pride remained committed to showcasing lighter weight classes within its regular events. Fighters who had previously competed in Bushido events were now given a platform alongside heavyweight stars. This integration allowed lighter-weight fighters to gain exposure to a broader audience, but it also meant they had to share the spotlight with Pride's more established divisions.

Pride's decision to discontinue Bushido and restructure its tournaments reflected a broader strategy to streamline operations and appeal to a global market. The promotion was already facing increasing competition from other MMA organizations, particularly the UFC. By consolidating its events and focusing on high-profile matchups, Pride hoped to maintain its position as a leader in the MMA world.

While the end of Bushido saddened many fans, it also provided an opportunity for the lighter weight classes to shine on a bigger stage. Fighters like Takanori Gomi and Shinya Aoki, who had become stars in Bushido, now had the chance to prove themselves in Pride's main events. This transition was not without its challenges, but it demonstrated Pride's commitment to evolving and adapting to the changing MMA landscape.

The restructuring of Pride's events also had an impact on its international presence. As Pride sought to expand its reach beyond Japan, integrating lighter weight classes into its main events made its shows more diverse and appealing to fans worldwide. This strategy aligned with Pride's broader goal of becoming a truly global MMA promotion, capable of competing with the UFC and other rising organizations.

Ultimately, the discontinuation of Bushido and the shift in Pride's tournament strategy marked a turning point for the promotion. It was a period of both opportunity and uncertainty, as Pride navigated the challenges of maintaining its reputation while adapting to a rapidly changing industry. The decisions made during this time would have a lasting impact on Pride's legacy and the future of mixed martial arts.

The Legacy of Bushido's End and Pride's Restructuring

The conclusion of Bushido events marked a significant shift for Pride, and the impact of this decision echoed throughout the MMA world. By integrating lighter weight classes into its main events, Pride attempted to broaden its appeal and streamline its offerings. This was a bold move, as Bushido had cultivated a unique identity and a dedicated fanbase. The decision to end the series left many fans nostalgic for its fast-paced, action-packed fights.

The cancellation of the lightweight Grand Prix, which was expected to launch Pride's new tournament format, was another blow. Fans had eagerly anticipated the opportunity to see the best fighters in the lightweight division compete on a global stage. The failure to deliver on this promise highlighted the challenges Pride faced in balancing innovation with operational stability.

Despite these setbacks, Pride's integration strategy provided opportunities for lighter-weight fighters to gain exposure alongside the promotion's heavyweights and middleweights. This shift allowed stars like Takanori Gomi to showcase their skills to a broader audience, helping to cement their legacies within the sport. However, it also posed challenges, as lighter-weight fighters had to compete for attention in an already crowded field.

Pride's efforts to restructure its events were part of a broader strategy to maintain its position as a premier MMA promotion. The organization was facing increasing competition from the UFC, which was rapidly expanding its reach and fanbase. By consolidating its events and focusing on global expansion, Pride aimed to remain relevant in a changing industry.

The integration of lighter weight classes into main events aligned with Pride's goal of creating a more inclusive and diverse promotion. This strategy also appealed to international fans, who appreciated the variety of talent showcased at Pride events. However, the loss of Bushido's distinct identity meant that some fans felt the promotion had lost an essential part of what made it unique.

As Pride continued to evolve, it faced the challenge of balancing tradition with innovation. The decision to discontinue Bushido and restructure its tournaments reflected the organization's commitment to adapting to new realities. However, it also underscored the difficulties of maintaining a cohesive identity while pursuing growth and expansion.

The end of Bushido and the introduction of a new tournament cycle were turning points in Pride's history. These changes were driven by the need to address financial pressures, operational challenges, and increasing competition. While these decisions were not without controversy, they demonstrated

Pride's determination to navigate the complexities of the MMA industry.

In the years that followed, the legacy of Bushido and Pride's restructuring efforts continued to influence the sport of mixed martial arts. The lessons learned during this period served as a reminder of the challenges and opportunities inherent in the pursuit of excellence. Pride's story, including its bold decisions and occasional missteps, remains a testament to the resilience and creativity that define the world of MMA.

Part Four: The Zuffa Takeover and a New Chapter

Chapter 13: The Zuffa Acquisition of Pride (2007)

In March 2007, the mixed martial arts world was shaken by the announcement that Zuffa, the parent company of the Ultimate Fighting Championship (UFC), had acquired Pride Fighting Championships. Lorenzo Fertitta, co-owner of Zuffa, spearheaded the deal to purchase all Pride assets from Dream Stage Entertainment (DSE). The deal, reportedly valued at $65 million, transferred ownership of Pride's video library, fighter contracts, and brand rights to a new entity, Pride FC Worldwide Holdings, LLC.

The acquisition was framed as a way to unify the best MMA talent globally. Fertitta and Zuffa executives planned to continue promoting Pride events in Japan while integrating fighters into the UFC, envisioning cross-promotional "super fights" between stars of both organizations. This dream of unifying MMA under a single global umbrella excited fans and fighters alike, but it also raised concerns about maintaining the distinct identity of Pride.

Despite the optimistic plans, challenges quickly arose. The Pride brand was deeply rooted in Japanese culture, with its unique production style and strong fanbase. Replicating this magic under foreign ownership proved daunting. Language barriers and cultural differences complicated the transition, and questions lingered about whether Zuffa could maintain the respect and credibility Pride had built in Japan.

In the months following the acquisition, Zuffa began to assess the logistics of running Pride. Prominent

Pride executives, including Nobuyuki Sakakibara, stepped away from the organization, leaving a leadership void. Without the original team's deep connections to Japanese broadcasters and sponsors, Zuffa faced difficulty securing deals that could sustain Pride's operations in its home market.

Another complication was Pride's reputation for connections with the Yakuza, Japan's organized crime syndicates. While DSE denied these allegations, they cast a shadow over Pride's marketability, especially in Japan's corporate sphere. Broadcasters and advertisers became hesitant to associate with the promotion, further complicating Zuffa's efforts to revitalize the brand.

Despite these hurdles, Zuffa moved forward with integrating Pride's fighter roster. Contracts were reviewed, and negotiations began to bring stars like Fedor Emelianenko, Wanderlei Silva, and Shogun Rua into the UFC. However, these efforts weren't always successful. Fedor, one of Pride's biggest draws, did not sign with the UFC due to disagreements over contract terms, which was a significant loss in the eyes of fans.

The much-anticipated Pride 34: Kamikaze became the promotion's final event under DSE. Held in April 2007, it featured a nostalgic lineup of top fighters but lacked the energy and grandeur of Pride's peak years. For fans, it marked the end of an era. While Zuffa had initially intended to host additional Pride-branded events, logistical and financial challenges soon led to the abandonment of these plans.

By the end of 2007, Pride had effectively ceased operations. The UFC absorbed many of its fighters and used Pride's legacy to build its reputation as the premier MMA organization. Although the acquisition ended Pride's standalone presence, its influence remained significant. The fighters, events, and culture of Pride left an indelible mark on MMA history.

The story of Pride's acquisition by Zuffa was both a milestone and a cautionary tale in MMA. While it brought the sport closer to unification, it also highlighted the challenges of preserving a unique brand identity in the face of globalization. Pride's legacy lives on in the memories of its fans and the fighters who showcased their skills on its grand stage.

The Zuffa Acquisition of Pride

The acquisition of Pride Fighting Championships by Zuffa marked the end of an era for mixed martial arts. It was a bold attempt to unify the sport under a single, global organization. However, the transition was anything but smooth, and its aftermath highlighted both the potential and the challenges of such a monumental deal.

When Zuffa purchased Pride, the initial excitement revolved around the possibility of dream matchups between Pride and UFC fighters. Fans envisioned epic battles that would settle long-standing debates about which organization had the superior talent. Despite this, only a few of these matchups ever materialized. Fighters like Rampage Jackson and Shogun Rua transitioned successfully to the UFC, but others, such as Fedor Emelianenko, remained out of reach due to contractual disagreements.

Cultural and operational differences further complicated Zuffa's plans. Pride had thrived on its theatrical presentation and unique connections to Japanese culture. Zuffa's attempts to replicate this magic faltered without the original team's knowledge and networks. As a result, the Pride brand struggled to maintain its identity and appeal under new management.

The allegations of ties between Pride and the Yakuza proved to be a significant barrier. While Zuffa worked to distance itself from these accusations, the damage to Pride's reputation in Japan was already done. Sponsors and broadcasters hesitated to invest in the promotion, cutting off crucial revenue streams and limiting its chances of survival.

Financially, the deal brought mixed outcomes. While Zuffa gained access to Pride's video library and fighter contracts, the expected profits from operating Pride in Japan did not materialize. Efforts to host additional Pride events outside of Japan also faced challenges, ultimately leading to the quiet dissolution of the brand.

Pride 34: Kamikaze was a bittersweet farewell to the organization's glory days. Although the event featured some of Pride's most beloved fighters, it lacked the energy and pageantry that had defined earlier events. For fans, it was a poignant reminder of what had been lost in the pursuit of expansion and unification.

Despite these struggles, Pride's legacy endured. Its fighters became integral to the UFC, raising the level of competition and introducing a global audience to the unique style and spirit of Japanese MMA. Additionally, Pride's influence could be seen in the evolution of MMA's rules, production values, and international reach.

In the years following the acquisition, the MMA world reflected on the significance of Pride's rise and fall. It was a story of ambition, innovation, and the complex dynamics of cultural and corporate integration. While Pride's brand no longer existed as an independent entity, its impact on the sport remained profound.

The acquisition of Pride by Zuffa was a turning point in MMA history. It signified both the opportunities and the challenges of unifying a fragmented sport. Pride's legacy lived on not just in the fighters who carried its banner, but in the memories of fans who experienced its unmatched spectacle.

Chapter 14: Operating Pride Separately

After the acquisition of Pride by Zuffa in 2007, Lorenzo Fertitta emphasized that the organization would not simply be absorbed into the UFC. Instead, Pride was to continue operating as a separate brand, keeping its distinct identity intact. Fertitta compared the situation to the AFL-NFL merger in American football, where the leagues initially maintained their independence but eventually came together for epic championship games. This vision aimed to create crossover opportunities that would excite fans worldwide.

Fertitta's plan included keeping Pride events in Japan to preserve the strong connection to its original fanbase. He acknowledged the unique cultural elements that had made Pride successful, such as its dramatic production style, enthusiastic crowds, and the reverence shown to fighters. Pride's distinct rules, including the use of a ring instead of a cage and soccer kicks, were also to remain part of its identity.

A key aspect of the strategy was the idea of hosting "crossover" events between Pride and UFC fighters. These matchups would showcase the best talent from each organization, generating significant buzz and answering long-debated questions about which roster had the superior fighters. The promise of dream matchups like Wanderlei Silva versus Chuck Liddell became a focal point of fan discussions.

Despite the ambitious plans, logistical and operational challenges soon emerged. Running Pride as a separate entity required maintaining the infrastructure and relationships that had supported it in Japan. However, many of Pride's staff and partners did not transition to Zuffa, creating gaps in expertise and connections. These challenges were compounded by the lingering damage to Pride's reputation from the Yakuza allegations.

The crossover events also faced complications. While some fighters were enthusiastic about the idea, others were tied up with existing contracts, injuries, or personal disputes. Organizing these high-profile matches proved to be more difficult than anticipated, delaying the realization of Fertitta's vision.

Meanwhile, the UFC was experiencing rapid growth in North America. As its popularity surged, Zuffa's focus increasingly shifted toward expanding the UFC brand, leaving less attention and resources for Pride. The initial excitement around maintaining Pride as a separate organization began to wane as the logistical and financial hurdles mounted.

Although some crossover fights eventually happened, they did not occur under the Pride banner. Instead, Pride's roster was gradually integrated into the UFC, with stars like Rampage Jackson, Shogun Rua, and Anderson Silva achieving great success in their new organization. Pride itself ceased to operate as an independent entity, and its unique elements faded away.

Despite the challenges, Fertitta's vision highlighted the potential for unity in the MMA world. While Pride could not sustain itself as a separate brand, its fighters and legacy became an integral part of the sport's evolution. The idea of cross-promotion lives on as a reminder of what could have been, inspiring fans and promoters alike to dream of a unified MMA landscape.

The story of Pride under Zuffa is a tale of ambition, obstacles, and adaptation. It serves as a reminder that even with the best intentions and resources, preserving a legacy requires more than just financial investment. Pride's spirit lives on in the memories of its fans and the fighters who continue to represent its legacy in the octagon.

The Unrealized Vision of Pride's Independence

The announcement of maintaining Pride as a separate entity was met with excitement and high hopes. Fans were eager to see the two brands coexist, offering diverse styles and events while also delivering dream matchups. However, the vision proved far more challenging to execute than initially expected. Despite the enthusiasm from fans and fighters, reality presented hurdles that gradually led to the merger's ultimate outcome.

One of the significant challenges was preserving Pride's identity. Its dramatic entrances, unique rules, and distinct production style were cornerstones of its appeal. However, recreating these elements under Zuffa's management, especially outside Japan, was complicated. Many key staff members from Pride's original organization did not transition, leading to a loss of expertise and cultural understanding.

Another issue was logistical. While the idea of crossover events sounded thrilling, making them happen required navigating contract disputes, injuries, and promotional hurdles. Fighters from both organizations expressed interest in proving themselves, but setting up these matchups required time and careful negotiation, which often clashed with Zuffa's focus on rapidly growing the UFC.

Financial concerns also played a role. Pride's reputation had been damaged by allegations of organized crime ties, and sponsors were wary. The loss of Japanese television deals further strained its viability as a separate entity. Zuffa had to weigh the costs of operating Pride against the increasing success of the UFC, which was experiencing unprecedented growth in North America.

As time went on, Zuffa's priorities shifted. The UFC became the focal point, drawing the best fighters from Pride's roster into its fold. Stars like Rampage Jackson, Mauricio "Shogun" Rua, and Wanderlei Silva transitioned into the UFC and made significant impacts, but their battles no longer carried the Pride banner.

The dissolution of Pride marked the end of an era in MMA. While the organization's events had captured the imagination of fans around the world, its decline highlighted the complexities of running an international sports promotion. Even with Zuffa's resources, maintaining Pride's independence proved unfeasible in the face of cultural, logistical, and financial challenges.

Nevertheless, Pride's legacy lives on. The fighters who competed in its ring became legends, inspiring new generations of athletes. Its tournaments and events are still celebrated as milestones in MMA history, remembered for their intensity and drama. The spirit of Pride Fighting Championships remains alive in the hearts of fans and fighters alike.

The vision of Pride as a standalone brand may not have materialized, but its influence is undeniable. It brought MMA to new heights, showcasing the beauty of the sport on a global stage. While Pride as an organization ceased to exist, its ethos continues to resonate, reminding everyone of the passion and excitement that made it extraordinary.

Chapter 15: Uncertain Future for Pride

After the sale of Pride Fighting Championships to Zuffa was finalized on May 25, 2007, fans and fighters were left wondering about the future of the iconic MMA organization. While Zuffa initially hinted at keeping Pride as a separate entity, subsequent remarks by spokesperson Dana White cast significant doubt on these plans. White's comments suggested that instead of maintaining Pride, Zuffa was more focused on absorbing Pride's star fighters into the UFC.

White emphasized the challenges of sustaining Pride in Japan. One of the biggest hurdles was securing a new television deal, a critical factor for any promotion's success. Despite efforts to rebuild Pride's presence in Japan, White openly stated that local networks were resistant to working with Zuffa. He remarked, "I've pulled every trick out of the box, but I can't get a TV deal over there." Without television coverage, the chances of Pride regaining its former glory seemed slim.

The focus soon shifted to integrating Pride's fighters into the UFC roster. This process began almost immediately, with major stars like Quinton "Rampage" Jackson, Mirko Cro Cop, and Antônio Rodrigo Nogueira making their UFC debuts. Fans were excited to see how these fighters would perform in the Octagon, but it became clear that Pride as a brand was being sidelined.

Another obstacle to reviving Pride was its tarnished reputation in Japan. Allegations of ties to organized crime had damaged the promotion's credibility, making it even harder for Zuffa to secure sponsorships and partnerships in the region. Zuffa's ownership brought hope for a fresh start, but the lingering controversies proved difficult to overcome.

By late 2007, Zuffa's priorities had shifted entirely toward expanding the UFC. The organization was growing rapidly in the United States and internationally, and the resources needed to resurrect Pride were redirected to UFC's global development. The dream of crossover events between Pride and UFC fighters began to fade as Zuffa focused on consolidating its fighters under the UFC banner.

Pride's final event, Pride 34: Kamikaze, became a symbolic farewell to the organization. Fighters and fans alike celebrated the legacy of Pride, but the absence of future events left a void in the MMA world. For many, Pride represented a unique era of martial arts, blending entertainment with elite competition.

Despite its closure, Pride's influence on MMA cannot be overstated. The fighters who competed in its ring went on to achieve legendary status, and its events set new standards for production and drama. Pride's rules, tournaments, and memorable moments remain a cherished part of MMA history.

While Zuffa's acquisition marked the end of Pride as an independent entity, its spirit lives on through the fighters and fans who continue to celebrate its legacy. The story of Pride is one of triumph, innovation, and resilience, leaving an indelible mark on the sport of mixed martial arts.

The End of an Era for Pride

The uncertainty surrounding Pride Fighting Championships after its acquisition by Zuffa marked the end of a historic chapter in MMA. Despite initial promises to maintain Pride as a separate entity, the reality became increasingly clear—Pride's days as a standalone promotion were numbered. Dana White's candid remarks about the challenges of reviving Pride in Japan revealed the difficulties Zuffa faced in reestablishing its presence. The absence of a television deal in Japan was a crippling blow, and without that vital support, Pride's operations were unsustainable.

Zuffa's strategy quickly shifted toward absorbing Pride's talent into the UFC. This integration allowed fans to witness dream matchups between fighters who had previously competed in separate organizations. While this was an exciting prospect, it also signaled the end of Pride as a unique brand. Fighters like Wanderlei Silva, Dan Henderson, and Fedor Emelianenko became central to the narrative of transitioning Pride's legacy into UFC's growing empire.

One of the most significant challenges in reviving Pride was overcoming its tarnished reputation in Japan. The allegations of yakuza ties not only cost Pride its Fuji TV contract but also eroded trust among sponsors and fans. Zuffa inherited these challenges, and despite their best efforts, the organization could not rebuild the bridges needed to sustain Pride in its homeland. Pride's credibility issues were too deeply rooted to recover fully.

The cancellation of the 2007 lightweight Grand Prix was another indication that Pride's operations were winding down. For years, the Grand Prix tournaments had been a highlight of Pride's calendar, showcasing the best fighters in thrilling formats. Their absence left fans with a sense of loss, as the tournaments had been a cornerstone of Pride's identity.

Pride's closure was not just the end of a promotion but also the end of an era that defined a distinct style of MMA. The iconic white ring, soccer kicks, and yellow cards were all trademarks that set Pride apart from its competitors. These elements created an atmosphere that felt as much like a spectacle as a sport. For fans and fighters alike, Pride represented a unique blend of artistry and athleticism.

Zuffa's decision to focus on the UFC's growth was a logical business move, but it left many Pride loyalists feeling bittersweet. The UFC's expansion into global markets was undeniably successful, yet it came at the cost of Pride's dissolution. As the UFC became the dominant force in MMA, the diversity of promotions that had once characterized the sport diminished.

Pride's legacy, however, remains intact. The memories of epic battles, unforgettable events, and legendary fighters continue to inspire MMA fans worldwide. Pride was more than just a promotion—it was a phenomenon that brought martial arts to new heights. Its influence can still be seen in today's MMA, from the fighters it produced to the techniques and strategies it popularized.

Though Pride Fighting Championships is no longer active, its impact will never be forgotten. Its rise and fall tell a story of ambition, innovation, and resilience, leaving a lasting imprint on the sport of mixed martial arts. For those who experienced the magic of Pride, its legacy is not just history but a source of enduring inspiration.

Chapter 16: The Closing of Pride's Japanese Office

In October 2007, Pride's Japanese office was officially shut down, marking another chapter in the organization's decline. After the acquisition by Zuffa and the folding of Dream Stage Entertainment (DSE), many within the MMA community hoped that Pride could still operate under new management. However, the closure of the Japanese office proved otherwise, signaling that Pride's operations in its home country were coming to an end.

The office closure resulted in the layoff of 20 employees, many of whom had been with DSE during Pride's peak years. These individuals had worked tirelessly to build Pride into one of the most celebrated MMA promotions in the world. The decision to let them go reflected the harsh realities of the transition. Pride Worldwide, the entity created by Zuffa to manage Pride's assets, was focusing its efforts elsewhere, leaving little room for a continued presence in Japan.

For fans, this was a somber moment. The Japanese office had been the heart of Pride's operations since its inception, overseeing everything from event planning to fighter management. Its closure symbolized the dismantling of the infrastructure that had supported Pride's rise to prominence. The loss of these dedicated workers further distanced Pride from its origins, transforming it from a vibrant organization into a mere collection of assets under Zuffa's control.

This move also highlighted the challenges Zuffa faced in operating Pride as a separate entity. Without strong local connections and the infrastructure that the Japanese office provided, it became increasingly difficult to maintain Pride's unique identity. Additionally, the lack of a television deal in Japan made it unfeasible to stage events in the country, which had been the core of Pride's operations.

The closure of the office was a reflection of the broader struggles faced by Zuffa in attempting to revive Pride. Despite acquiring the brand and its assets, Zuffa encountered numerous obstacles, from legal and reputational issues in Japan to the logistical challenges of managing an international promotion. The layoff of employees was a pragmatic step, but it was also a clear indication that Pride would not be returning to its former glory.

For the Japanese MMA community, the closure of Pride's office was a major loss. Pride had been a cultural phenomenon in Japan, drawing massive crowds and showcasing the best fighters from around the world. Its events were not just competitions; they were spectacles that celebrated martial arts. The end of Pride's operations in Japan left a void that no other promotion could fully fill.

The employees who were let go faced an uncertain future. Some moved on to other roles within the MMA industry, while others left the sport altogether. Their contributions to Pride's success were invaluable, yet they became casualties of the promotion's decline. This was a poignant reminder of the human cost of Pride's collapse, as the passion and dedication of these workers were overshadowed by business decisions.

Ultimately, the closure of the Japanese office marked the beginning of the end for Pride as a brand. While

Zuffa continued to integrate Pride's fighters and assets into the UFC, the spirit of Pride—its unique style, culture, and identity—was left behind. The legacy of Pride Fighting Championships would live on in the memories of fans and fighters, but its physical presence in Japan was now a thing of the past.

A Symbolic End for Pride's Operations

The closure of Pride's Japanese office in October 2007 marked a significant turning point for the organization. This step was not just about ending an administrative hub—it symbolized the final unraveling of Pride Fighting Championships as a standalone entity. Despite initial promises to preserve Pride's identity, the decisions made after its acquisition by Zuffa reflected a gradual dismantling rather than revitalization.

For many, this closure felt like the end of an era. The Japanese office had been the backbone of Pride's operations, hosting the passionate team that orchestrated some of MMA's most memorable events. With the layoff of the remaining staff, the possibility of staging future events in Japan dwindled further. This loss wasn't just practical; it carried emotional weight for fans who saw Pride as more than a business—it was a cultural phenomenon that put Japanese MMA on the global map.

Zuffa faced challenges that were not easily overcome. The lack of a television deal in Japan hampered their ability to rebuild Pride locally, and logistical hurdles made maintaining a dual-promotion model unsustainable. As a result, Pride's resources, fighters, and legacy became absorbed into Zuffa's primary brand, the UFC. While some fighters found new opportunities, others saw their careers stalled amid the uncertainty surrounding Pride's future.

The closure also left an emotional gap for the Japanese audience. Pride's events weren't just about fights; they were grand spectacles that celebrated martial arts traditions and showcased international talent. The cultural impact of Pride went beyond MMA, blending sport with entertainment in a way that resonated deeply with fans. With the office shut down, this unique approach to MMA seemed to fade along with the organization.

This moment also highlighted the difficulties in translating Pride's success into the new ownership structure. Pride had thrived on its distinctly Japanese ethos, but under Zuffa's management, it struggled to retain this identity. The closure of the Japanese office was a clear sign that Pride would no longer be able to operate as it once had. Instead, its essence was gradually folded into the UFC, leaving behind a sense of nostalgia for what could have been.

The employees who were laid off faced the harsh reality of Pride's decline. Many had worked tirelessly during Pride's peak years, contributing to its reputation as one of the greatest MMA organizations in history. Their departure was a poignant reminder of the human cost of this transition. While Zuffa continued to benefit from Pride's assets, the people who helped build the brand were left to move on.

For fans, this chapter in Pride's story was bittersweet. The memories of incredible matches, legendary fighters, and electrifying events remained vivid, but the organization itself was no longer the powerhouse it once was. The closure of the office in Japan felt like an official end, a moment where hope for Pride's revival dimmed entirely.

In the years that followed, Pride's influence could still be seen in MMA's global evolution, but its unique character was irreplaceable. The closure of its Japanese office marked the conclusion of a journey that had begun with so much promise and excitement. While Pride's legacy endures, this moment will always be remembered as the final step in the organization's decline.

Part Five: Pride Beyond the Ring – The Multimedia Expansion

Chapter 17: Pride's Legacy Through Video

Pride Fighting Championships' legacy didn't end with live events; its matches and fighters found new life through video media. After the final Pride events, a series of DVDs were released under the Pride Worldwide label, ensuring that fans could relive some of the greatest moments in MMA history. These DVDs captured the excitement and unique energy of Pride, becoming popular collectibles among MMA enthusiasts worldwide.

In 2010, Pride's content gained a fresh audience with the launch of *Best of Pride Fighting Championships* on Spike TV. Hosted by Kenda Perez, the program showcased some of the most memorable fights and highlights from Pride's archives. By presenting the matches to a broader audience, Spike TV allowed new fans to experience the high-quality production and international talent that set Pride apart.

The series highlighted classic matchups, dramatic rivalries, and the evolution of mixed martial arts during Pride's peak years. Fighters like Fedor Emelianenko, Wanderlei Silva, and Kazushi Sakuraba continued to captivate audiences through these broadcasts, solidifying their legendary status. The show also served as an introduction to Pride's unique atmosphere, from the respectful Japanese crowd to the dramatic entrances and high-stakes competition.

Streaming platforms and online video services further expanded access to Pride's catalog. Fans could watch iconic bouts on-demand, helping to maintain Pride's reputation as a pioneer in the sport. These digital platforms brought Pride to younger generations, many of whom were too young to watch the events live during their original broadcasts.

The availability of Pride's fights on video also played a significant role in shaping MMA culture. Aspiring fighters studied the techniques and strategies showcased in Pride, while fans analyzed the bouts to better understand the evolution of the sport. Pride's influence extended beyond Japan and the United States, reaching audiences across Europe, South America, and beyond.

Video games also helped carry Pride's legacy. Titles like *Pride FC: Fighting Championships* for the PlayStation 2 allowed fans to immerse themselves in the Pride experience by controlling their favorite fighters. The game captured the essence of Pride's unique rule set and aesthetic, further cementing its place in MMA history.

The preservation of Pride's matches on video is a testament to its enduring impact. Even years after its final event, Pride continues to inspire and entertain through these visual archives. The sport of MMA owes much of its growth to Pride, and the availability of its fights ensures that its legacy will not be forgotten.

Through video media, Pride Fighting Championships remains a vital part of the MMA world. Its fights, fighters, and unforgettable moments live on, connecting past, present, and future generations of fans. Video has proven to be a powerful tool in keeping the spirit of Pride alive, allowing its influence to resonate far beyond its final bell.

Pride's Legacy Lives On Through Video

Pride's presence in the world of MMA has continued to resonate long after its final events. The release of its events on DVD allowed fans to relive the drama, excitement, and iconic battles that defined the organization. These DVDs became essential for MMA enthusiasts, showcasing the best fighters and legendary moments in Pride's history. Through these releases, Pride maintained its influence, ensuring its events were not forgotten by a new generation of fans.

The introduction of "Best of Pride Fighting Championships" on Spike TV in 2010 marked another milestone in preserving Pride's legacy. Hosted by Kenda Perez, the program provided viewers with a curated look at some of the organization's most memorable fights. For many fans, this show was a gateway into the world of Pride, introducing them to the explosive energy and technical brilliance that made it a global phenomenon.

What made "Best of Pride" special was its accessibility. By airing on Spike TV, Pride's historic fights reached a wider audience, including those who might not have been familiar with its impact. The program celebrated the artistry of the fighters and gave fans a deeper appreciation for the skill and dedication that went into each bout.

The use of video to keep Pride alive is a testament to the power of storytelling. Each match was more than a fight; it was a narrative of rivalries, triumphs, and heartaches. Through video, fans could connect with these stories, feeling the emotions that defined the Pride experience.

Pride's video legacy also highlighted its role in shaping modern MMA. Fighters who rose to fame in

Pride, such as Fedor Emelianenko, Wanderlei Silva, and Mirko Cro Cop, became household names, inspiring countless fighters worldwide. The visual documentation of their journeys ensured their contributions were celebrated for years to come.

Moreover, these videos served as a time capsule, capturing an era when MMA was still finding its identity. Pride's unique rules, presentation, and unmatched atmosphere were forever immortalized, giving fans a glimpse into a chapter of MMA history that can never be replicated.

The enduring popularity of Pride's video content proves that its impact transcends time. Fans continue to share and celebrate its fights on social media, forums, and YouTube, keeping the spirit of Pride alive. The memories of Pride remain vivid, not just for its legendary fighters but also for the way it redefined combat sports entertainment.

Through its video archive, Pride Fighting Championships has cemented its place as a cornerstone of MMA history. Its ability to connect with fans, even years after its closure, underscores the lasting legacy of an organization that changed the landscape of the sport forever.

Chapter 18: Pride in Gaming

Pride Fighting Championships expanded its influence beyond live events, broadcasting, and video archives by entering the world of video games. This move allowed fans to immerse themselves in the Pride experience, engaging with its iconic fighters and unique style in an interactive format. Through these games, Pride created a bridge between the world of combat sports and gaming, solidifying its cultural footprint in an entirely new medium.

Releasing licensed video games was a smart way to extend the reach of Pride's brand. These games allowed fans to relive classic battles or create dream matchups that never happened in real life. Players could control legendary fighters, utilizing moves and techniques that mirrored the high-level skills seen in actual Pride bouts. This immersive experience brought fans closer to the action, giving them a taste of what it was like to compete on the Pride stage.

Video games also helped Pride attract a younger audience. While many fans discovered Pride through live broadcasts or DVDs, gaming provided another point of entry. Younger audiences, especially those already interested in martial arts or MMA, could experience the thrill of Pride fights firsthand through the games. This interaction helped keep the Pride legacy alive for new generations of fans.

The games celebrated the essence of Pride Fighting Championships, showcasing its vibrant presentation, international roster of fighters, and dynamic ruleset. They brought to life the energy of a packed Saitama Super Arena, complete with the signature pageantry and atmosphere that made Pride events unique. Fans could hear the roar of the crowd and feel the tension of each fight, capturing the spectacle that made Pride so memorable.

Pride's entry into gaming also served as a historical record of its roster and events. By featuring fighters from its golden era, the games became a snapshot of Pride's greatest moments. This documentation preserved the legacy of both the fighters and the organization, ensuring their impact on the sport would not fade with time.

In addition to extending its legacy, Pride's video game ventures provided a platform for storytelling. Players could follow the journeys of their favorite fighters, imagining themselves as champions battling for glory. These games celebrated the personalities and rivalries that defined Pride, allowing fans to connect with the emotional side of the sport.

The release of Pride-themed games also underscored the global reach of the organization. By venturing into the gaming market, Pride acknowledged its diverse fanbase, many of whom were eager for ways to engage with the sport beyond watching events. This move demonstrated Pride's understanding of the growing popularity of MMA worldwide and its commitment to catering to its fans.

Even after Pride ceased operations, its impact in gaming remained significant. The games continued to serve as a reminder of Pride's legacy, with fans revisiting them to relive the magic of the organization. They became a gateway for new fans to discover Pride's history and a way for long-time followers to celebrate its unforgettable moments.

Through its video games, Pride Fighting Championships extended its legacy far beyond the arena, ensuring that its spirit lived on in the hearts and hands of gamers worldwide.

Pride's Digital Legacy

The release of video games by Pride Fighting Championships marked an important step in preserving its legacy and expanding its influence. These games were not just about entertainment; they symbolized Pride's commitment to connecting with fans in new and innovative ways. By moving into the digital realm, Pride ensured its essence and history would live on far beyond its final event.

Through the games, Pride became more than just an MMA promotion. It became a part of pop culture, immortalized in a way that books or documentaries alone could not achieve. The games allowed fans to participate in the action, creating a deeper and more personal connection to the fighters and the events. This interactivity kept Pride's spirit alive, even for those who never watched its events live.

Pride's foray into gaming also highlighted its forward-thinking approach. Understanding the growing influence of video games in popular culture, Pride embraced this medium as a tool to engage a younger and more global audience. The games acted as ambassadors, introducing new fans to the world of Pride and ensuring its rich history was not forgotten.

The visual and interactive nature of gaming gave fans a new way to experience Pride's excitement. Every punch, kick, and submission felt real, bringing the artistry of MMA into homes worldwide. The games captured the electric atmosphere of Pride events, complete with the dramatic entrances, intense rivalries, and unforgettable matchups.

Even after Pride ceased operations, its games remained a testament to its greatness. Fans returned to them to relive the organization's glory days, to play as their favorite fighters, and to remember the magic that was Pride. These games became time capsules, preserving Pride's essence for future generations.

The games also fostered a sense of community among fans. Online forums and discussions about strategies, fighters, and matchups brought people together, keeping Pride's legacy alive. The shared experiences of playing these games became part of what defined being a Pride fan.

In the end, Pride's venture into gaming was more than a business decision—it was a celebration of its identity. By translating its excitement, drama, and artistry into video games, Pride ensured it would always have a place in the hearts of its fans. Through these digital experiences, Pride's legacy continues to thrive, proving that its impact reaches far beyond the confines of the arena.

Pride's video games are a reminder of how powerful multimedia can be in preserving history. They stand as a tribute to the organization's boldness, creativity, and commitment to its fans. In the digital realm, Pride Fighting Championships remains undefeated.

Chapter 19: Pride FC: Fighting Championships – The First Game

Released in February 2003, Pride FC: Fighting Championships was the first video game based on the Pride Fighting Championships, developed by Anchor Inc. and published by THQ for the PlayStation 2. The game was available in Japan, North America, and Europe, allowing fans worldwide to engage with their favorite fighters in a virtual space. It featured a mix of realistic MMA action with simple controls and accessible gameplay, making it appealing to both casual players and hardcore fans of the sport.

One of the key features of Pride FC: Fighting Championships was its large roster of fighters. Players could choose from numerous Pride stars, including well-known names such as Wanderlei Silva, Kazushi Sakuraba, and Mark Coleman. The game allowed players to simulate famous Pride bouts, recreating the excitement of the real-life events. This was a major selling point for fans who wanted to relive the drama and intensity of the Pride events in their living rooms.

While the game aimed to capture the thrill of MMA, the controls were relatively simple. The player could perform basic strikes, grapples, and submissions, with a focus on timing and strategic execution. Despite the simplicity, the game did a decent job of delivering the essence of MMA, providing an enjoyable experience for both newcomers and seasoned players.

Critically, the game received mixed reviews, with an aggregate score of 73/100 on Metacritic based on 19 critic reviews. While the graphics were generally praised for their realistic representations of the fighters, some reviewers felt the gameplay lacked depth and variety. The lack of a robust single-player campaign and limited modes contributed to the criticism, as it didn't fully exploit the potential of the MMA genre. Still, for its time, it was a solid attempt at bringing Pride to a video game platform, giving fans a glimpse into what could be done with the sport in the digital world.

The graphics, while impressive for a PlayStation 2 game, showed signs of aging compared to later titles. The fighters were well-designed, but the animations could be stiff and repetitive at times. The game also featured the iconic Pride ring, a key part of the promotion's branding, which added to the authenticity. However, it was clear that Pride FC: Fighting Championships was still a product in its early stages, setting the foundation for future improvements.

Despite its shortcomings, the game did succeed in bringing Pride Fighting Championships to a new audience, helping to spread the popularity of MMA outside of the live events. It allowed fans to experience the sport in a new way and introduced them to the world of virtual fighting. It also served as a gateway to more complex MMA games in the future, including sequels and spin-offs that would expand on the formula laid out by this first entry.

The soundtrack in Pride FC: Fighting Championships also played a role in setting the tone of the game. The music selection matched the intense nature of the fights, keeping players engaged as they fought through various events. This helped build the atmosphere, giving players a sense of excitement and urgency as they progressed through each fight.

Pride FC: Fighting Championships marked the beginning of Pride's foray into the gaming world. It had its flaws, but it was a milestone in the promotion's legacy, offering a new way for fans to connect with the sport. It paved the way for future Pride games, pushing the boundaries of MMA in the digital space and solidifying the connection between Pride Fighting Championships and its dedicated fanbase. Though not perfect, it was a significant step in introducing MMA to the world of gaming.

Pride FC: Fighting Championships – The First Game

Pride FC: Fighting Championships was a groundbreaking release, marking the start of Pride's presence in the video game world. It brought the world of mixed martial arts into the hands of fans, allowing them to play as their favorite fighters in a way that was previously impossible. While the game's release in 2003 was met with mixed reviews, it was still an important step in bringing Pride Fighting Championships and the sport of MMA to a wider audience.

Despite receiving a variety of critiques, the game had several standout features. It allowed players to experience the excitement of Pride events by controlling top fighters like Wanderlei Silva and Mark Coleman. It was one of the first games to showcase MMA, and its realistic representation of the sport, including the iconic Pride ring, helped set it apart from other fighting games at the time. However, the simplicity of the controls and the lack of depth in the gameplay left room for improvement, which would be addressed in future titles.

One of the most significant aspects of Pride FC: Fighting Championships was its accessibility. The controls were easy for new players to pick up, making it enjoyable for those unfamiliar with MMA. However, seasoned fans might have found the gameplay lacking in complexity and variety, especially in comparison to later entries in the genre. This balance between accessibility and depth helped the game appeal to a broader audience, even if it fell short in certain areas.

The graphics were also impressive for the time. While not groundbreaking by today's standards, the character models and the attention to detail in the fighters' appearances helped enhance the realism of the game. The soundtrack played an essential role as well, helping to establish an intense atmosphere that matched the energy of real Pride events. All these elements combined to offer an immersive experience for fans of MMA and Pride, even if it wasn't perfect.

At the same time, the game's limited modes and lack of a compelling single-player campaign were significant drawbacks. The gameplay was focused mainly on individual fights, which didn't offer the depth and progression that fans would expect from more mature sports simulation games. This gap was noted by critics, and it was clear that Pride FC: Fighting Championships was not the final word in MMA gaming, but rather a stepping stone toward future developments in the genre.

Despite its limitations, Pride FC: Fighting Championships contributed to the growth of the MMA gaming community. It brought Pride's roster of fighters to new fans who might not have had access to the live events. It also introduced MMA to a broader gaming audience, setting the stage for future games that would improve upon the formula established in this first effort.

The game's impact extended beyond just entertainment. It served as a platform for fans to engage more deeply with Pride Fighting Championships, allowing them to experience the action of the sport from the comfort of their homes. This helped build the global fanbase for MMA and solidified Pride's place in the history of combat sports.

Pride FC: Fighting Championships was an important milestone for Pride and MMA in the world of video games. While it had its flaws, the game laid the foundation for future developments and served as an introduction to the world of MMA for many players. As the first Pride game, it's remembered as a significant step forward in bringing mixed martial arts to a wider audience, helping to shape the future of MMA gaming and the Pride legacy in the digital world.

Chapter 20: The Second Game – PrideGP Grand Prix 2003

PrideGP Grand Prix 2003 was the second video game based on the Pride Fighting Championships, and it was developed by Capcom, a company well-known for its expertise in creating engaging fighting games. Released in November 2003, the game was available for the PlayStation 2, but it was only released in Japan. This was a notable decision, as fans outside of Japan had to import the game to play it, which limited its exposure to a global audience compared to its predecessor.

The game's development focused on creating a more refined and immersive experience, building upon the foundation established by Pride FC: Fighting Championships. Capcom made significant efforts to improve the game mechanics, enhancing the combat system and adding new features to keep the gameplay fresh. The game allowed players to control real-life Pride fighters in various tournament modes, with a particular emphasis on the 2003 Grand Prix events.

PrideGP Grand Prix 2003 featured a roster of fighters from the Pride Fighting Championships, including popular names like Wanderlei Silva, Fedor Emelianenko, and Kazushi Sakuraba. The game aimed to replicate the excitement of the real-life tournament, where players could experience the thrill of competing in a high-stakes fighting event. The game also included several customization options, allowing players to modify their fighter's appearance and skills.

One of the key features of the game was its presentation. The developers ensured that the arenas and fighter animations were as realistic as possible, capturing the atmosphere of a live Pride event. The music and sound effects were also carefully chosen to enhance the player's immersion, further contributing to the overall experience. Although the game was limited to the Japanese market, it still garnered attention from fans abroad who were eager to experience the game and support the Pride brand.

Despite its limitations, PrideGP Grand Prix 2003 received positive reviews for its gameplay and attention to detail. Critics praised the game's depth and the wide variety of fighters available. However, some players found that the game was somewhat challenging, with a steep learning curve for those unfamiliar with the mechanics of fighting games. Even so, the game's dedication to faithfully recreating the Pride Fighting Championships events made it a hit among fans.

The game's reception was generally favorable, though it wasn't as widely recognized as other fighting games in the global market. Nonetheless, it contributed to the growing popularity of the Pride brand and served as an important part of the Pride Fighting Championships' legacy. The game continued to showcase the unique style of MMA promoted by Pride, and it further solidified the connection between video games and real-world sports entertainment.

In terms of its impact, PrideGP Grand Prix 2003 set the stage for future games based on MMA and combat sports. Its success proved that there was a market for MMA-based video games, and it inspired other companies to pursue similar projects. The game also helped introduce a new generation of fans to the sport of MMA, particularly those who may not have had access to the live events or televised broadcasts.

Looking back, PrideGP Grand Prix 2003 holds a special place in the history of Pride Fighting Championships video games. While it may not have achieved the same level of international recognition as other games in the genre, it remains a beloved title among fans who appreciate the nostalgia and the effort put into making it an authentic representation of the Pride Fighting Championships brand.

PrideGP Grand Prix 2003

PrideGP Grand Prix 2003 marked a significant milestone in the history of Pride Fighting Championships' video game adaptations. Developed by Capcom and released in Japan, the game built upon the foundation set by its predecessor, Pride FC: Fighting Championships. While it was only available in Japan, the game's release was a testament to the growing popularity of mixed martial arts (MMA) and the Pride brand during that time.

The game showcased the 2003 Grand Prix tournament and allowed players to control famous fighters such as Wanderlei Silva and Fedor Emelianenko. This was a major draw for fans of the sport, as they could recreate the excitement of the real-life events in the virtual world. The developers paid great attention to detail in the game's presentation, ensuring that the arenas, fighter animations, and sound effects all contributed to an immersive experience. This dedication to realism made the game appealing to both MMA fans and video game enthusiasts.

In terms of gameplay, PrideGP Grand Prix 2003 offered a more refined experience than its predecessor, with improved mechanics and new features. Players could customize their fighters, which added an extra layer of personalization to the game. However, the difficulty level of the game was a point of contention for some players. Newcomers to the genre found the learning curve challenging, but the game's depth and variety of available fighters were still highly appreciated.

The game's reception was generally positive, with critics praising its accuracy in replicating the atmosphere of the Pride events. While it may not have reached the same level of worldwide recognition as other fighting games, it still gained a loyal following, especially in Japan. PrideGP Grand Prix 2003 also had a lasting impact on the MMA video game market, as it demonstrated that there was a demand for MMA-based games. This success paved the way for future titles in the genre.

Despite being confined to the Japanese market, the game had a significant influence on the popularity of Pride Fighting Championships, particularly with fans who were looking for a way to experience the action outside of the live events. The game helped extend the reach of Pride, especially for international fans who might not have had access to the fights through traditional channels. It also showcased the potential of MMA video games, which would later lead to the creation of many more titles based on the sport.

Looking back, PrideGP Grand Prix 2003 holds a special place in the hearts of fans who remember the golden era of Pride Fighting Championships. It was not just a video game, but a way for fans to engage with the sport they loved in a new and exciting way. While the game may not have been widely available outside Japan, it contributed to the lasting legacy of Pride and solidified its place in the history of combat sports video games.

PrideGP Grand Prix 2003 was an important chapter in the Pride Fighting Championships' history. It helped introduce the world of MMA to a broader audience, especially in the gaming community, and it offered fans a chance to experience the excitement of Pride's Grand Prix tournaments. Even though it was a niche title, it remains a beloved game among MMA enthusiasts and Pride fans. The game's impact was felt not just in the gaming world, but also in the broader landscape of combat sports, where it continues to be remembered as one of the pioneering MMA video games.

Chapter 21: Pride in UFC Undisputed 3

In 2012, Pride Fighting Championships made its return to the world of video games with a feature in UFC Undisputed 3, a game developed by Yuke's and published by THQ. This addition marked a significant moment for fans of Pride, as it allowed players to experience the iconic Pride events and fighters in a new, updated format. The game introduced a dedicated Pride mode, bringing the essence of the original Pride Fighting Championships to life within the UFC universe.

UFC Undisputed 3 featured a robust selection of 33 Pride fighters, including legends like Wanderlei Silva, Fedor Emelianenko, and Mirko Cro Cop. These fighters, alongside the Pride ruleset, created a unique experience that distinguished the Pride mode from the UFC portion of the game. The inclusion of Pride events allowed fans to relive the excitement and spectacle that made the original promotion famous. Players could step into the ring with fighters who were once household names in the world of MMA, including those who transitioned to the UFC in later years.

One of the standout features of the Pride mode in UFC Undisputed 3 was the inclusion of Pride-specific rules. Fighters could compete under the iconic Pride event rules, which included elements such as yellow cards for stalling, as well as the familiar ring instead of the UFC's octagon. This attention to detail gave players an authentic Pride experience, as it captured the special atmosphere that set the organization apart from others. The rules were central to the game mode and added a level of strategy that appealed to both hardcore fans and newcomers to the MMA gaming scene.

The commentary in UFC Undisputed 3 also contributed to the authenticity of the Pride mode. Bas Rutten, a former MMA fighter and commentator, and Stephen Quadros, known for his work with Pride events, provided commentary that added a sense of nostalgia for fans of the promotion. Their voices brought back memories of the excitement that fans experienced when watching live events. In addition, the game featured Lenne Hardt as the English ring announcer and Kei Grant as the Japanese ring announcer, faithfully replicating the atmosphere of a live Pride event. These contributions helped elevate the game's presentation, making it a true celebration of Pride Fighting Championships.

While UFC Undisputed 3 allowed players to fight under Pride rules and with Pride fighters, it also created a bridge between the two organizations. Many of the Pride fighters in the game had already made their mark in the UFC, allowing fans to experience the crossover between the two brands. This crossover was especially significant given the history of the two organizations and their shared fighters. Players could match Pride legends against UFC stars, creating dream matchups that once seemed impossible. This feature expanded the game's appeal to a wider audience, offering something for fans of both promotions.

Despite the addition of Pride to UFC Undisputed 3, the game was not only a nostalgia trip for longtime fans of Pride Fighting Championships but also an opportunity for newer fans to discover the promotion's rich history. The inclusion of Pride fighters and events brought a new dimension to the UFC Undisputed series, enriching the experience for players who were already familiar with the UFC's current roster. The game acted as a sort of time capsule, preserving the legacy of Pride while integrating it with the modern MMA landscape.

For those who missed the original Pride events, UFC Undisputed 3 provided an invaluable opportunity to experience them in a virtual setting. The game allowed fans to relive key moments from Pride's history, such as the fierce rivalry between Wanderlei Silva and Quinton "Rampage" Jackson, or the dominance of Fedor Emelianenko in the heavyweight division. These moments, though part of the past, continued to live on in the game, making it a meaningful tribute to the Pride era.

Ultimately, the inclusion of Pride in UFC Undisputed 3 was a way for the gaming community to honor the impact of Pride Fighting Championships on the MMA world. The game offered a well-rounded, immersive experience that highlighted the unique qualities of Pride, from its rules to its fighters and presentation. Even though the Pride brand was no longer active in the real world, its legacy continued to influence the sport of MMA and was preserved for a new generation of fans through UFC Undisputed 3.

The feature of Pride Fighting Championships in UFC Undisputed 3 was a remarkable moment for MMA fans. It served as a bridge between the past and present, allowing fans to experience the best of both worlds. With its faithful recreation of Pride rules, its iconic roster of fighters, and the inclusion of commentary from the voices of Pride itself, the game was an exceptional tribute to a promotion that helped shape the future of MMA.

Pride in UFC Undisputed 3

The inclusion of Pride Fighting Championships in UFC Undisputed 3 marked an important moment for both fans of the UFC and Pride, blending the rich history of the Japanese promotion with the modern landscape of mixed martial arts. By offering a dedicated Pride mode, the game provided a way to celebrate the iconic fighters and events that made Pride a standout organization in the early years of MMA's global rise. For longtime fans, this was a special moment that allowed them to experience Pride events and fighters once again, while younger players got their first look at a promotion that had shaped the sport.

The Pride mode in UFC Undisputed 3 allowed players to immerse themselves in the unique rules and atmosphere that set Pride apart from other promotions. The inclusion of the ring, yellow cards for stalling, and the full set of Pride rules helped to preserve the essence of the promotion and gave fans the opportunity to experience the excitement of the old days. These features set Pride apart from the UFC and made the mode stand out in the game, allowing players to experience the distinctive qualities of Pride in a way that was faithful to its original format.

The game's roster of 33 Pride fighters was another highlight. Legends such as Wanderlei Silva, Fedor Emelianenko, and Mirko Cro Cop brought their unique fighting styles to the game, offering a diverse set of fighters for players to choose from. The inclusion of these fighters allowed fans to relive some of the most memorable moments from Pride's history, such as Silva's legendary rivalries and Emelianenko's reign as one of the most dominant fighters of his time. Even though the promotion was no longer active, these fighters' presence in the game kept their legacy alive.

One of the key aspects of UFC Undisputed 3's Pride mode was the use of commentary from figures closely associated with Pride's history. Bas Rutten and Stephen Quadros, both known for their work in Pride events, provided commentary that added authenticity to the gameplay experience. Their familiar voices brought back the feeling of watching live events, enhancing the game's atmosphere. Additionally, the inclusion of Lenne Hardt and Kei Grant as the ring announcers in their respective languages helped to further replicate the Pride experience, from the dramatic entrances to the high-energy fights.

UFC Undisputed 3 also allowed players to pit Pride fighters against UFC stars, which was a dream matchup for many fans. This crossover between the two organizations was a significant moment in MMA history, as it represented the merging of two distinct eras. For fans of both Pride and the UFC, this provided a unique opportunity to see what would have happened if these two organizations had ever truly collided in the ring.

Despite Pride no longer being an active promotion at the time of the game's release, UFC Undisputed 3 kept the spirit of the brand alive. By including fighters, rules, and commentary from Pride, the game allowed players to experience what made Pride so special and ensured that its impact on the sport of MMA was not forgotten. For those who had followed Pride during its prime, the game offered a nostalgic trip down memory lane, while younger fans had the chance to explore the history of one of MMA's most influential promotions.

The addition of Pride in UFC Undisputed 3 also contributed to the game's overall success. The feature appealed to both UFC and Pride fans, offering a diverse range of content that extended the game's replay value. By including a mix of classic Pride content and UFC matchups, the game satisfied a broad audience and provided a comprehensive MMA experience. It became a celebration of MMA history, bridging the gap between the two major promotions.

Ultimately, UFC Undisputed 3's Pride mode served as a fitting tribute to the lasting impact of Pride Fighting Championships. It gave players a chance to revisit the glory days of the promotion, even if only in a virtual setting, and allowed the next generation of fans to experience its rich legacy. By preserving the essence of Pride in the game, the developers ensured that the impact of the promotion on the sport of MMA would continue to be felt long after its closure. The Pride mode in UFC Undisputed 3 helped solidify the place of Pride Fighting Championships in the history of mixed martial arts, ensuring that its influence would live on in the digital world.

Part Six: The Rules That Defined Pride

Chapter 22: Pride's Rules

Pride Fighting Championships had a distinctive set of rules that helped shape the unique identity of its events. These rules were particularly notable when compared to other MMA promotions, and they varied between main Pride events and the smaller Bushido events. One of the most well-known aspects of Pride's rules was its emphasis on stand-up fighting, which encouraged more dynamic action in the ring. Unlike the UFC, where fighters could be separated for inactivity and brought back to their feet, Pride often allowed the fighters to continue fighting on the ground unless there was clear inactivity.

Pride events featured a ring rather than a cage, and this influenced the rules significantly. The fighters were required to fight in a ring, where there were no corners as seen in cage-based fights. This design encouraged more movement and less stalling, as fighters could not use the corners to escape or recover in the same way. While this setup made for exciting, fast-paced bouts, it also posed some challenges, as it provided fewer opportunities for fighters to lean on the cage for defense or strategy.

Another key difference was the time rounds. In Pride, most fights had three five-minute rounds. However, Pride's Bushido events, which focused on lighter weight classes, had different rules. The Bushido format featured a unique scoring system, where the rounds were divided into one 10-minute round and one 5-minute round. This rule change was introduced to encourage fighters to maintain a faster pace and prevent stalling. It was considered one of the ways to make the fights more exciting for fans, particularly in the lighter weight classes.

One of the most distinctive rules in Pride was the yellow card system. This system was used to penalize fighters for stalling or avoiding action in the ring. If a fighter was deemed to be stalling by the referee, they would receive a yellow card, which resulted in a deduction from their purse. This system was controversial but effective in encouraging active fighting, especially in situations where fighters would be content to wait out the clock without engaging fully. This was a major difference from the UFC, which relied more heavily on the referee's discretion to separate fighters and restart the action.

The rules of Pride also allowed soccer kicks and stomps to the head of a downed opponent, which were not allowed in most other MMA promotions. This created an added element of danger for fighters, as a single kick or stomp to the head of a grounded opponent could end the fight quickly. While these techniques were controversial, they were a key part of the Pride identity and often led to some of the most memorable moments in the organization's history. Fighters had to constantly be aware of their positioning, knowing that a mistake could cost them the fight.

However, in 2006, Pride made a significant announcement that the Bushido events would be discontinued. This was a direct response to the changing landscape of mixed martial arts, as Pride sought to streamline its focus and integrate the lighter weight classes back into the main Pride events. The decision to end the Bushido series was part of a broader effort to unify the organization and create a more consistent brand. The rules for the main Pride events and Bushido events had become increasingly similar, leading to the eventual merger.

Despite the discontinuation of Bushido events, the legacy of Pride's unique rules continued to have a significant impact on the MMA world. Many of the techniques and ideas introduced in Pride, like the yellow card and the use of the ring, were carried over to other promotions. Pride's influence on the sport remained long after the organization's closure, as fighters and fans alike appreciated the action-packed style of fighting that Pride had pioneered.

In the end, Pride's rules were a reflection of the company's commitment to delivering exciting, high-energy fights. From the ring to the time limits to the yellow card system, each aspect of the rules was designed with one goal in mind: to entertain. Even after the organization closed, Pride's legacy of innovative rules and thrilling action left a lasting mark on the MMA world. These rules defined the sport during its prime, and they remain a beloved part of Pride's legacy to this day.

Legacy of Pride's Rules: Shaping MMA's Future

The rules of Pride Fighting Championships were central to the organization's identity and success. From its early years, Pride differentiated itself from other MMA promotions by creating a unique set of guidelines that enhanced the viewing experience. These rules were designed to encourage active and dynamic fighting, and many of them became integral parts of what fans came to expect from the promotion. The use of a ring instead of a cage was one of the most distinct features, affecting how fighters approached their matches. The absence of cage control made the fighters rely more on movement, which led to more exciting exchanges and less stalling.

The time structure of Pride events was also a defining characteristic. While most promotions followed a simple three-round format, Pride introduced variations, particularly in the Bushido events. These lighter-weight events featured a 10-minute first round followed by a 5-minute second round, which was intended to create a faster pace and force the fighters to engage more quickly. This rule was particularly appealing to fans who preferred the quick, high-energy battles often associated with the lighter weight divisions.

Another important rule in Pride was the yellow card system, which helped eliminate stalling in fights. If a fighter engaged in inactivity or failed to engage in action, they would receive a yellow card. This card resulted in a deduction from the fighter's purse, ensuring that they remained active throughout the match. The introduction of this rule showed Pride's commitment to keeping the fights fast-paced and thrilling. Unlike the UFC, which often relied on the referee's discretion, the yellow card system provided a clear, quantifiable way to penalize fighters for not staying active.

Pride's allowance of soccer kicks and stomps to the head of a downed opponent was another rule that set it apart from other organizations. These techniques were dangerous but added a layer of excitement and intensity to the fights. Fighters had to be constantly aware of their positioning to avoid taking a potentially fight-ending blow to the head. While controversial, the inclusion of these techniques became part of the signature style of Pride and contributed to the promotion's reputation for brutal and thrilling combat.

The decision to discontinue Bushido events in 2006 marked a significant shift in Pride's strategy. With the lighter weight classes being integrated back into the main Pride events, the organization sought to streamline its operations and focus on its most successful format. This move demonstrated Pride's adaptability in an ever-changing market, responding to shifts in fan preferences and the evolving landscape of MMA. Despite the discontinuation of Bushido, many elements of the original series, like the unique time structure and the emphasis on faster fights, remained in the main events.

Though Pride was eventually absorbed by Zuffa, the rules that were introduced during its years in operation had a lasting influence on the MMA world. Many aspects of Pride's fighting style, such as the ring, the active fighter penalties, and the emphasis on excitement, became widely adopted in other promotions. Fans and fighters alike appreciated these aspects, which provided a unique, high-energy experience that set Pride apart from other MMA organizations.

Pride's rules were more than just guidelines—they were a reflection of the promotion's core philosophy. The organization sought to create fights that were fast, exciting, and full of action. The distinctive rules, including the yellow card system, the ring, and the allowance of certain dangerous techniques, played a large role in shaping the style of fighting that Pride became known for. Even after its closure, the impact of these rules continued to resonate in the world of MMA, with many of them still being considered a hallmark of what makes the sport thrilling. Pride's approach to rules was innovative and remains a significant part of its legacy in mixed martial arts.

Chapter 23: Match Length

Pride Fighting Championships used a unique match structure that differed from many other MMA promotions. The standard Pride match consisted of three rounds. The first round was ten minutes long, and the second and third rounds were each five minutes. This structure set Pride apart from organizations that typically used three five-minute rounds for all non-title fights. Intermissions between rounds in Pride events were two minutes long, giving fighters some time to recover before continuing the battle.

However, when Pride hosted events in the United States, they adopted the Unified MMA rules used by the Nevada State Athletic Commission (NSAC). In these events, non-title matches were shortened to three five-minute rounds, with title fights lasting five five-minute rounds. The intermissions between rounds were reduced to one minute for these matches, providing a quicker turnaround between rounds compared to the standard Pride format. This shift reflected the regulatory standards of the U.S., aiming to keep the event in line with other local promotions.

Grand Prix events, which were a hallmark of Pride's history, had their own unique format for match length. When two rounds of a Grand Prix took place on the same night, the first round of each match lasted ten minutes, while the second round was five minutes. This format made the Grand Prix a thrilling spectacle, as fighters had to compete in longer rounds, testing their endurance and strategy. The intermissions between rounds in Grand Prix bouts were also two minutes, maintaining the standard Pride event format.

The decision to have a ten-minute first round was part of what made Pride events distinctive. This longer round allowed fighters to settle into their rhythm, create more dynamic strategies, and potentially tire out their opponents before the shorter rounds began. Many fans appreciated the change in pace, as it often led to more exciting and action-packed bouts. Fighters had to be more tactical, using the extra time in the first round wisely, as the shorter rounds that followed required quicker bursts of energy.

The standard match length was seen as a test of stamina and mental toughness, and it became a significant part of Pride's identity in the MMA world. The longer first round allowed fighters to showcase their endurance, and it also set the stage for dramatic comebacks and memorable moments. This structure encouraged fighters to think strategically, conserving their energy during the longer first round and planning for the intensity of the following rounds.

In contrast, other MMA organizations typically used shorter rounds, which created a faster-paced but more intense competition. The Pride format gave fighters more opportunities to adapt during the fight, and it helped elevate certain styles of fighting, particularly those that relied on grappling and ground control. Some fighters thrived under these rules, while others struggled with the endurance required to perform well in a longer first round.

The structure of Pride matches also allowed for dramatic narratives to unfold during events. Fighters who could last through the long first round had a better chance of adjusting to their opponent's style, especially in the high-pressure environment of a Grand Prix. This allowed fans to see fighters at their best and often brought out the true depth of their fighting skills.

Pride's match length format influenced MMA as a whole, with the longer rounds becoming a part of the sport's rich history. The unique structure of Pride events helped build the promotion's legacy, and it remains a point of discussion among MMA fans and analysts. While other organizations may have changed their format, the memory of Pride's distinctive approach to match length endures as a key part of what made their events unforgettable.

The Pride Match Format and Its Legacy

Pride Fighting Championships' match length format helped define its identity and set it apart from other MMA promotions. The unique structure of having a ten-minute first round followed by two five-minute rounds created a distinct rhythm for each fight. This allowed for longer strategy sessions in the first round, giving fighters a chance to test their endurance and skills before entering the shorter, more intense rounds. The standard two-minute intermissions allowed fighters to recover, adding to the dramatic feel of each event.

The difference in match lengths between Pride events and those in the United States highlighted the flexibility of the sport. In U.S. events, following NSAC Unified MMA rules meant shorter rounds, with only one-minute breaks in between. This increased the pace and intensity, leading to faster exchanges and less room for prolonged strategy. While some fans preferred this quicker format, others enjoyed the unique pacing of the Pride events, which allowed for a more calculated and methodical approach to fighting.

The Grand Prix format, which featured longer first rounds, further distinguished Pride's style. Fighters had to adapt quickly to the extended first round, making it an interesting challenge for those known for their fast-paced aggression. It also meant that fighters with strong endurance could shine, while those who struggled in longer bouts might have to adjust their game plans to stay competitive.

The use of a longer first round in Grand Prix events allowed fans to witness more complex strategies, as fighters had more time to adjust to their opponent's tactics. Some matches developed a more measured pace, with fighters who were skilled in ground control or grappling benefiting from the extra time. This added depth to the competition, making it less about raw speed and more about skill, endurance, and adaptability.

The strategic elements of Pride's format played a big role in its success. Fighters learned how to conserve energy, create opportunities, and capitalize on their opponent's mistakes. The longer first round allowed for more tactical maneuvers, especially in the grappling department, which helped shape the evolution of MMA fighting styles. Fighters like Wanderlei Silva, Fedor Emelianenko, and Mauricio "Shogun" Rua thrived under the longer match structure, showcasing a combination of power and strategy that helped elevate their careers.

Pride's format also offered unique advantages for fighters with exceptional stamina. Those who could last through the ten-minute first round were often better prepared for the shorter rounds that followed, as they had already gauged their opponent's strategy and tested their own endurance. This dynamic kept the competition exciting, especially in high-stakes tournaments like the Grand Prix, where fighters were expected to compete multiple times in one night.

Despite the differences between Pride's match length and other organizations, it became a signature part of Pride's legacy. The longer first round added a sense of depth and strategy to each fight, providing a rich contrast to other organizations that favored faster-paced bouts. Fans continued to appreciate the difference, and it became one of the defining aspects of Pride's appeal.

Looking back, Pride's match length rules played a significant role in shaping the promotion's place in MMA history. The format allowed for more strategic fights, helping establish Pride as a powerhouse in the sport. While the rules might not have been universally loved, they certainly contributed to the legendary moments and unforgettable matches that continue to be remembered by MMA fans worldwide. The match length structure remains a vital part of the Pride legacy and a key feature that set it apart in the world of mixed martial arts.

Chapter 24: Weight Classes

In Pride Fighting Championships, weight classes were structured differently compared to many other organizations. While most MMA promotions strictly divide fighters based on weight, Pride allowed more flexibility. A fighter could be booked to fight an opponent of any weight, and it was not unusual to see matchups between fighters from different weight classes. This created a unique dynamic and often led to exciting and unpredictable bouts. The flexibility in matchmaking allowed Pride to put together many thrilling fights that would not have happened under more rigid weight class systems.

The weight divisions in Pride were primarily used for championship bouts and in Grand Prix tournaments to determine the best fighter in a particular weight class. This approach added an extra layer of intrigue to the tournaments, as the best in each division would compete for the title. In some ways, this allowed for more exciting matchups, as fighters from different weight classes could be pitted against each other, creating interest from fans who wanted to see how certain styles matched up.

The lightweight division in Pride had a weight limit of 73 kg (161 lb) and was introduced in 2004. This division allowed for the lighter, faster fighters to showcase their skill set, often focusing on speed, technique, and precision. Fighters in this division were known for their fast-paced style and ability to capitalize on openings with quick strikes and dynamic grappling techniques.

The welterweight division followed the same path, with a weight limit of 83 kg (183 lb), also introduced in 2004. This weight class allowed fighters who were not quite in the middleweight class but still heavier than the lightweights to compete at a high level. Welterweight fighters had the advantage of strength and power while still retaining the agility and speed that were key to their success in the division.

The middleweight division, with a limit of 93 kg (205 lb), had been part of Pride since 2000. This was one of the most popular weight classes, as many of the biggest names in Pride competed in this division. Fighters in the middleweight category were often well-rounded, with the ability to strike powerfully and grapple effectively. This made for some of the most entertaining and competitive fights in Pride history.

The heavyweight division, with no weight limit, had been a cornerstone of Pride since its early days in 2000. It was home to some of the biggest and most dominant figures in MMA, including Fedor Emelianenko and Mirko Cro Cop. Without a weight restriction, the heavyweight division allowed for an open playing field, where fighters of all sizes could compete against each other. This made for some highly anticipated and intense battles, as fighters with vastly different body types and skill sets squared off.

Pride also introduced the concept of openweight bouts, starting in 1997. In openweight fights, there were no weight restrictions, allowing fighters from any division to face off. These fights were particularly interesting because they pitted fighters of vastly different sizes and styles against one another. The openweight format often led to dramatic matchups that fans would eagerly anticipate, as there was always the potential for the underdog to pull off an upset.

The flexible approach to weight classes in Pride created a unique atmosphere in the sport. Fighters were not limited by rigid divisions, and the possibilities for exciting, cross-weight matchups were endless. This helped set Pride apart from other promotions and made it one of the most innovative and entertaining organizations in MMA history. The emphasis on talent over strict weight restrictions allowed for a diverse range of fighters to thrive, regardless of their size, and this contributed to Pride's lasting impact on the sport.

Final Thoughts on Pride's Weight Classes: A Legacy of Flexibility and Innovation

The weight classes in Pride Fighting Championships played a crucial role in shaping the organization's identity and the exciting dynamics of its events. Unlike other organizations that strictly separated fighters based on weight divisions, Pride embraced flexibility, allowing fighters to face opponents of different weights. This unique approach often led to unpredictable and exciting matchups, capturing the attention of fans around the world. The emphasis on talent and skill over rigid weight divisions created a diverse and engaging atmosphere for both fighters and spectators.

One of the standout features of Pride was its ability to mix different styles and body types within the same event, giving fans a variety of fighting techniques to enjoy. With no strict adherence to weight class restrictions, Pride produced some of the most memorable fights in MMA history, where strength, agility, and technique were tested in ways that were difficult to predict. This flexibility also allowed for the creation of unique events, like the openweight bouts, where fighters from any weight class could compete against each other, regardless of size.

The lightweight division, introduced in 2004 with a 73 kg (161 lb) weight limit, provided an outlet for some of the fastest and most skilled fighters in the sport. These athletes focused on speed, precision, and technical ability, bringing a different style of fighting compared to the heavier divisions. Their matches were characterized by fast-paced exchanges and dynamic grappling, which kept the fans on the edge of their seats.

The welterweight division, also introduced in 2004, offered a middle ground between the lighter and heavier divisions. Fighters in this weight class, with a limit of 83 kg (183 lb), were known for their versatility. They combined strength and power with the agility needed to keep up with lighter opponents. This combination made the welterweight division one of the most competitive and exciting in Pride's history, with many memorable bouts that showcased the fighters' well-rounded skill sets.

Pride's middleweight division, which had a weight limit of 93 kg (205 lb), was home to some of the sport's biggest stars. Many of the most iconic names in MMA competed in this category, creating a deep pool of talent and rivalries. The middleweight class became known for its balance of speed, strength, and technique, producing a style of fighting that was accessible and entertaining to fans, regardless of their level of familiarity with the sport.

The heavyweight division, which had no weight limit, was one of Pride's most defining features. With the freedom for fighters of all sizes to compete, this division became a battleground for some of the most dominant athletes in the sport, including Fedor Emelianenko, Mirko Cro Cop, and others. The lack of weight restrictions allowed for the clash of giants and often produced highly anticipated matches where the fighters' raw power and heart were on full display.

In addition to the standard weight classes, the openweight bouts provided fans with something truly unique. These matches featured fighters from any division, often resulting in extreme mismatches that added an element of unpredictability to the sport. The openweight format created opportunities for upsets and provided a stage for underdogs to shine, creating some of the most thrilling moments in Pride's history.

Ultimately, Pride's approach to weight classes set it apart from other organizations in the MMA landscape. The organization's flexibility allowed fighters to showcase their talents without the constraints of a traditional weight class system. This open-minded approach to matchmaking helped create some of the sport's most unforgettable events, and Pride's influence on MMA can still be felt today. The variety of matchups and the emphasis on skill and heart rather than strict weight divisions made Pride a unique and beloved chapter in the history of mixed martial arts.

Chapter 25: The Pride Ring

Pride Fighting Championships used a unique and distinct ring design that became an iconic part of its events. Unlike the UFC, which typically uses an octagon, Pride used a square ring. This five-roped square ring had sides that measured 7 meters, or approximately 23 feet in length. This ring size was consistent for both major Pride events and the smaller Bushido events.

The design of the ring was integral to the Pride experience. The ropes were positioned higher than in most other combat sports rings, and the design was meant to allow for more fluid movement and action. Fighters could move around the ring freely, using the ropes for leverage or cornering opponents. The ring was part of Pride's identity, giving the organization its own distinct feel.

The Pride ring also had a larger central space for the fighters, compared to the standard ring found in other promotions. This extra space contributed to the sense of openness and allowed fighters to be more dynamic with their striking and grappling. It also made it easier for them to move around without feeling cramped or confined.

While the UFC's octagon has its advantages for control and ground fighting, Pride's square ring encouraged a different style of fighting. The ropes allowed fighters to use clinches and walls, creating a more versatile environment for all types of fighters. The open nature of the Pride ring meant that fights often saw more exchanges, as athletes were encouraged to engage rather than be forced into corners or held along the cage.

This ring style was a key part of Pride's brand. From the spectacle of the events to the excitement of the matches, everything about the ring contributed to the overall atmosphere. The ropes were not just a physical element but became part of the drama and intensity that Pride was known for. Fans around the world associate the square ring with some of the best moments in mixed martial arts history.

During Grand Prix tournaments, the ring was sometimes a key factor in determining strategy. Fighters would often try to position themselves against the ropes or use them to avoid being taken down. The lack of a cage meant that fighters had more freedom to move around, but it also meant they had to be aware of the ropes, which could be both an advantage and a disadvantage.

Another unique feature of the Pride ring was its lack of a cage. The absence of the cage allowed the fighters to focus solely on the action, with no interference from the confines of a metal structure. This made the fights feel less like a battle for control of the cage and more about pure combat. It gave Pride a distinct vibe that was different from other promotions at the time.

Pride's use of a five-roped square ring set it apart from other MMA organizations. The 7-meter squared ring created a sense of openness that allowed for dynamic exchanges, strategic movement, and unforgettable moments. For fans and fighters alike, the Pride ring became an essential part of the brand, contributing to its status as one of the greatest MMA promotions in history.

The Legacy of Pride's Ring: A Symbol of Combat

The Pride Fighting Championships' five-roped square ring left a lasting impact on the world of mixed martial arts. It wasn't just a physical structure; it became an emblem of the Pride brand itself. The 7-meter squared ring allowed for a dynamic fighting environment, encouraging fluid movement and constant action. Fighters had the freedom to move and engage, without the constraints of a cage, making for a unique experience for both competitors and fans.

One of the standout features of the Pride ring was its height and spacing of the ropes. Higher ropes allowed athletes to use them to their advantage, adding a new layer to strategy. Fighters could use the ropes to resist takedowns, execute moves against opponents, or even recover from being cornered. This flexibility contributed to the fast-paced and unpredictable nature of Pride events. It was a ring that facilitated action, making the promotion stand out from others that used the traditional cage.

The Pride ring was integral in shaping the way fights played out. Its spacious design encouraged fighters to use the entire area, making it ideal for both striking and grappling. While the UFC's octagon created a more controlled environment, the Pride ring allowed for more fluid exchanges, creating space for both techniques. This open structure meant that fighters had to think on their feet, constantly aware of the ropes and how to use them.

The absence of a cage also changed the way the fighters approached their matches. The lack of the usual confinement meant there was no battleground for control of the cage. It gave a sense of freedom, allowing the fighters to focus purely on their opponent and the fight at hand. In contrast to the more defensive tactics used in the octagon, Pride's square ring encouraged a more offensive mindset.

Another interesting aspect of the Pride ring was its role in Grand Prix tournaments. During these events, the ring's unique design played a significant part in the strategies that fighters used. Fighters often had to adapt their game plans to the space available, knowing the ropes could either be a help or a hindrance. The open ring provided a fresh challenge for the competitors, making Grand Prix matches even more thrilling to watch.

For fans, the Pride ring was an essential part of the spectacle. The ring was not just a place where fights occurred but a backdrop to some of the most memorable moments in MMA history. From dramatic knockouts to hard-fought decisions, the Pride ring witnessed some of the sport's greatest matches. The sound of the crowd, the movement of the fighters, and the tension in the air all added to the excitement.

The ring's design contributed to the promotion's identity. It wasn't just a place for fighting, but a symbol of Pride's unique approach to MMA. It reflected the organization's emphasis on innovation and high-energy bouts. The square ring became as synonymous with Pride as the fighters themselves, creating a legacy that continues to be celebrated.

The five-roped square ring was more than just a piece of equipment; it was a crucial part of what made Pride Fighting Championships special. Its design allowed for flexibility, strategy, and nonstop action. The unique structure encouraged fighters to engage, creating thrilling matchups that captured the attention of fans around the world. For many, the

Pride ring will forever remain a symbol of the promotion's innovative and exciting approach to MMA.

Chapter 26: Fighters' Gear and Attire in Pride

In Pride Fighting Championships, fighters had a great deal of freedom when it came to their choice of attire. While there were some mandatory elements, such as open-finger gloves, mouthguards, and a protective cup, fighters could personalize their appearance more than in some other organizations. This flexibility allowed them to bring their own style to the ring, while still meeting the basic safety requirements necessary for competition.

The primary attire that all fighters had to wear were the open-finger gloves. These gloves provided both protection and the ability to strike effectively. The open design allowed fighters to grip their opponents and execute submissions without losing the ability to strike with punches or elbows. This design became synonymous with mixed martial arts and was a staple of Pride's regulations.

In addition to the gloves, fighters were required to wear a mouthguard and a protective cup. The mouthguard helped protect the fighter's teeth and jaw, while also offering some level of protection against concussions. The protective cup, essential for safeguarding the groin area, was another mandatory piece of equipment. These two items were non-negotiable, ensuring the fighters' safety during the brutal exchanges that took place in the ring.

Beyond these required items, fighters were free to wear additional gear at their discretion. This included knee pads, elbow pads, ankle supports, or even wrestling shoes. For those coming from a grappling or wrestling background, wearing wrestling shoes could provide a significant advantage in terms of traction and mobility. Similarly, knee pads and elbow pads were useful for protecting joints during intense bouts.

Fighters could also choose to wear a gi top or gi pants, depending on their preference. While Pride was primarily a promotion focused on no-gi MMA, fighters who had a background in Brazilian jiu-jitsu or judo often chose to wear these items. The gi could be helpful in submission grappling, as it provided additional grips and control over an opponent. However, these choices were not always mandatory and depended on the individual fighter's approach to the sport.

Another unique aspect of Pride's attire regulations was the allowance for fighters to wear masks. While not common, some fighters chose to wear masks as part of their persona or to make an impression on the audience. These masks, though checked by referees before the fight for safety, became part of the fighters' personal identity. This level of individuality made Pride stand out, as it allowed competitors to express themselves through their gear.

Before every fight, the referee would inspect the fighters to ensure that their attire complied with Pride's rules. This was to ensure that all gear, whether it was a gi, elbow pads, or knee braces, was securely worn and didn't pose any potential hazards during the fight. The safety of the competitors was a priority, and each piece of equipment was checked thoroughly before the action began.

Pride Fighting Championships offered its fighters a unique level of freedom when it came to their attire.

While safety items like gloves, mouthguards, and protective cups were mandatory, fighters could personalize their appearance with optional equipment such as knee pads, gi tops, and even masks. This approach added a level of individuality to the competition, allowing fighters to showcase their personal style while still adhering to the safety standards necessary for MMA. This flexibility in attire was part of what made Pride a memorable and unique promotion in the world of combat sports.

A Fighter's Identity in the Ring

Pride Fighting Championships allowed fighters to showcase not only their skills but also their personality through the gear they chose to wear. This freedom in attire gave fighters a unique opportunity to express themselves while adhering to the sport's safety standards. The regulation of mandatory items such as gloves, mouthguards, and protective cups ensured that safety was never compromised, but fighters were given enough leeway to bring a personal touch to their appearance.

The most essential gear in Pride was undoubtedly the open-finger gloves. These gloves became a symbol of mixed martial arts, allowing fighters to deliver powerful strikes while also maintaining the ability to lock in submissions. With this versatile piece of equipment, fighters could balance both stand-up and ground techniques, making it indispensable for their performance. This standard equipment was something that all fighters had to wear, establishing a common ground for the competition.

Mouthguards and protective cups were equally important for fighters' safety, serving to protect the most vulnerable parts of the body. Fighters in Pride, known for their fierce battles, needed these pieces of gear to reduce the risk of injury during intense exchanges. By making these items mandatory, Pride ensured that the fighters could focus on the fight itself, with less concern for the risks that come with competing at such a high level.

The range of optional equipment was where Pride truly distinguished itself. Fighters were encouraged to wear knee pads, elbow pads, and ankle supports, providing extra protection for their joints. This additional gear gave athletes a chance to better protect themselves from the wear and tear that often comes with the sport. Whether fighters chose to wear wrestling shoes for better grip or added other protective gear, it was clear that Pride understood the physical demands of MMA and sought to make safety a priority.

For some, the ability to wear a gi top or gi pants offered an opportunity to connect with their grappling roots. Pride may have been focused on no-gi MMA, but those with backgrounds in Brazilian jiu-jitsu or judo often preferred to fight in these traditional garments. This flexibility allowed for a mix of fighting styles, as competitors could use their gi to execute techniques that were integral to their form of martial arts.

Additionally, the option to wear masks added an element of flair and drama to the events. Fighters who wore masks were able to create a persona, adding to the spectacle of the event. Though this was not the norm, the ability to wear a mask or other distinctive attire contributed to the unique atmosphere of Pride events, where fighters were more than just athletes—

they were characters who engaged with the fans in a way that made each fight feel like an event in itself.

The inspections by referees before each match ensured that the fighters' attire adhered to Pride's regulations. This was done to maintain safety during the fight, ensuring that nothing could potentially cause harm to the fighters or interfere with the match. The consistent checks were a critical part of keeping the competition fair and focused, allowing fighters to perform at their best without the distraction of unsafe or inappropriate gear.

The attire regulations in Pride Fighting Championships were designed to allow for both individuality and safety. While there were basic mandatory items like gloves, mouthguards, and protective cups, the promotion gave fighters the freedom to express themselves with additional gear like gi tops, knee pads, and even masks. This flexibility contributed to Pride's distinct identity, allowing fighters to bring their full personalities into the ring while ensuring that safety and fairness were always the top priorities.

Chapter 27: The Fight for Victory

In Pride Fighting Championships, there were several ways a match could be won, giving fighters a variety of paths to victory. One of the most common ways to win was by submission. This happened when a fighter either tapped out three times on their opponent or the mat to signal surrender, or verbally submitted by saying they give up. Another way to win by submission was through technical submission, which could occur if a fighter went unconscious due to a choke or had a body part like an arm broken due to a submission hold. These types of victories were a testament to a fighter's ability to control their opponent and force them to give up.

Another key method of victory was knockout, or KO. This happened when a fighter was struck with a legal blow that caused them to fall to the ground and either become unconscious or unable to continue fighting. A knockout is one of the most dramatic ways to win a fight and often leads to an immediate finish. Fighters who could land a solid knockout punch or kick earned great respect in the sport, as it showed precision and power in their strikes.

In addition to knockout, there was the technical knockout, or TKO. A TKO occurred when the referee stopped the fight because one fighter was completely dominating the other to the point that the opponent was in danger. A TKO could also be declared if a doctor stopped the fight due to a legal injury sustained during the match. This rule helped protect the fighters and ensure their safety during particularly brutal bouts.

A fight could also be forfeited if a fighter's corner decided to throw in the towel, signaling that their fighter could no longer continue. This was often seen as a sign of a fighter's well-being being prioritized, as the corner crew would make the decision when they felt their fighter was taking too much damage or could no longer defend themselves adequately.

If a match reached its time limit without a decisive winner, the outcome was determined by the judges. In Pride, fights were scored in their entirety, meaning the entire fight was considered as a whole, rather than being judged round-by-round. In Pride events held in the United States, however, the fights were judged round-by-round. The judges made their decisions based on several factors, with the most important being the effort made to finish the fight via knockout or submission. Damage inflicted on the opponent, standing combinations, ground control, and aggressiveness also played key roles in scoring.

Weight differences could also factor into the decision. If there was a weight difference of 10 kg (22 lb) or more between the fighters, this could influence the judges' decision. This helped level the playing field and ensure that heavier fighters did not have an unfair advantage over their lighter counterparts. If a fight was stopped by a ring doctor after an accidental but illegal action like a clash of heads, and the fight was in the second or third round, the judges would determine the winner based on the same criteria.

In some cases, a fighter could be disqualified for illegal actions. A yellow card or green card was given as a warning if a fighter broke the rules or failed to follow the referee's instructions. If a fighter received three warnings, they would be disqualified from the fight. A fighter could also be disqualified if a match was stopped due to deliberate illegal actions, like a purposeful low blow. The use of substances such as oil, ointment, or cream on the body was prohibited, and if a fighter was caught using these substances, they would be disqualified.

In rare situations, a fight could be declared a "no contest." This occurred when both fighters committed violations of the rules or when a fight was stopped by a ring doctor due to an accidental illegal action, such as a clash of heads. If this happened during the first round, the match would be ruled a no contest. This ruling ensured that fights were fair and that the integrity of the sport was upheld, especially in cases where both fighters had been affected by the same violation.

Overall, Pride's victory rules were designed to create an exciting and fair environment where fights could be decided in a variety of ways. Whether through submission, knockout, decision, or disqualification, each victory told a different story, highlighting a fighter's skills and ability to perform under pressure. These rules ensured that the matches were as thrilling and competitive as possible, offering a wide range of outcomes for fans to enjoy.

The Fight for Victory

Victory in Pride Fighting Championships (Pride FC) could be achieved through various ways, each emphasizing the excitement and unpredictability of mixed martial arts (MMA). Whether through a powerful knockout, a skillful submission, or a referee stoppage, every win reflected a fighter's dedication, skill, and resilience. The detailed victory rules not only ensured fairness but also added a unique layer to the competition, making Pride FC stand out in the world of MMA.

Submission victories were often the result of a fighter's ability to control their opponent, forcing them into a position where they had no choice but to tap out. Whether it was a simple tap on the opponent or the mat three times, or a technical submission where the opponent passed out from a choke or suffered a broken limb, these moments were intense and often marked the end of a battle in the most decisive manner. The skill required to perform such submissions reflected the fighter's technical prowess, making such victories highly respected.

Knockouts were perhaps the most dramatic form of victory. When a fighter delivered a blow so powerful that their opponent fell unconscious or unable to continue, the crowd's energy reached a peak. A knockout was a clear sign of dominance, showing that a fighter could overpower their opponent with sheer force. Whether it was a punch, a kick, or another strike, knockouts were the fastest way to win and often became the most memorable moments in Pride FC history.

Technical knockouts (TKO) also played a significant role, where a referee or doctor called for a stoppage due to the severe damage one fighter inflicted on another. This could happen when one fighter was completely overwhelmed and unable to defend themselves effectively, or when a doctor decided that the fighter's injuries made it unsafe for them to continue. This method of victory highlighted the risks fighters took in the cage, showcasing their bravery while ensuring their safety.

When matches went to a decision, judges were tasked with scoring the fight based on specific criteria. The winner was determined by the fighter's effort to finish the fight, the damage they inflicted, their ground control, and overall aggressiveness. This system was designed to reward fighters who were active and sought a clear victory rather than merely avoiding defeat. It created a thrilling dynamic, where each fighter had to stay aggressive and tactical to impress the judges and secure a win.

Disqualifications and no contests were unfortunate outcomes, but they were essential to maintaining the integrity of the sport. A fighter's actions could lead to a disqualification if they committed an illegal action, like using prohibited substances or engaging in unsportsmanlike conduct. Similarly, a match could be declared a no contest if both fighters committed violations or if an accidental illegal action caused a fight to be stopped. These rules ensured that fighters respected both the sport and their opponents.

In Pride FC, the pursuit of victory was more than just a personal achievement—it was a testament to the fighter's journey, discipline, and respect for the sport. Each rule, each method of victory, added to the rich history of Pride, shaping the way MMA evolved. Fighters and fans alike understood that winning in Pride wasn't just about beating an opponent; it was about showcasing the heart, courage, and skill required to compete at the highest level of MMA.

Ultimately, Pride FC's victory rules were a crucial part of what made the organization unique in the MMA world. They balanced fairness with excitement, creating an environment where every fight mattered and every victory had a story to tell. These rules not only shaped the outcome of fights but also helped define the spirit of competition that Pride FC became known for, leaving behind a legacy in the world of mixed martial arts.

Chapter 28: Fighting Fair – The Rules Against Fouls

In Pride Fighting Championships (Pride FC), maintaining fairness and safety was a top priority, which is why they implemented strict rules against certain fouls. These fouls were actions that could put a fighter at risk of injury, undermine the integrity of the sport, or simply be unsportsmanlike. The goal was to ensure that fighters respected each other, the sport, and the audience by competing fairly and safely.

One of the most dangerous fouls in Pride FC was headbutting. A headbutt could cause serious damage to an opponent and is considered a reckless attack. It was banned because it often resulted in cuts, concussions, or even broken noses. The rules of Pride FC made it clear that no fighter was allowed to use their head as a weapon in the ring.

Eye gouging was another prohibited action, as it can cause lasting harm to a fighter's vision. Fighters were expected to avoid deliberately trying to damage their opponent's eyes. This rule was implemented to keep fighters safe from long-term injuries and preserve the integrity of the sport.

Hair pulling, biting, and fish hooking were all actions that could cause unnecessary pain or injury. These fouls were considered unsportsmanlike and dangerous. Hair pulling could lead to neck injuries or give one fighter an unfair advantage. Biting was seen as a sign of desperation and violence, while fish hooking – which involves pulling at the inside of an opponent's mouth – was not only painful but also unsafe.

Attacks to the groin, small joint manipulation, and strikes to the back of the head were also banned. Strikes to the groin could cause significant damage, while small joint manipulation, such as manipulating fingers or toes, could result in broken limbs. Punching the back of the head, particularly the occipital region and spine, was forbidden as well. These areas of the body were especially vulnerable to serious injury, and targeting them could lead to devastating consequences.

In Pride FC, purposely throwing an opponent out of the ring or running out of the ring was also considered a foul. These actions not only disrupted the flow of the fight but could also cause the fighters to become disoriented or injured. It was important for fighters to stay within the ring to maintain fairness and avoid creating dangerous situations.

Fighters were also not allowed to purposely hold onto the ropes. If a fighter hung an arm or leg on the ropes to gain an advantage or to prevent themselves from being thrown, the referee would immediately issue a warning. This rule was in place to prevent any unfair advantage gained from the ropes and keep the match competitive.

Finally, in Pride events held in the United States, stomps to a grounded fighter, along with kicks and knees to the head of a grounded opponent, were prohibited. These actions were seen as particularly dangerous, as the grounded fighter would have little defense against such strikes. However, in non-US Pride events, such techniques were allowed, showcasing how the rules differed depending on the location of the event.

If a fighter committed an illegal action that led to an injury, the referee and ring doctor would assess the situation. If the injured fighter needed time to recover, the round would pause, and once the fighter was ready, the match would resume from the exact point it was stopped. However, if the injury was too severe for the fighter to continue, the one responsible for the foul would be disqualified. This strict rule helped maintain safety and discipline in the sport.

These fouls and their strict penalties helped Pride FC establish itself as an organization that valued fairness, safety, and respect for its fighters. While MMA is a violent sport, the rules set in place by Pride ensured that the violence remained within the boundaries of competition, protecting fighters from harm and keeping the sport both exciting and fair.

The Fight for Fairness – Protecting the Athletes

In Pride Fighting Championships, the rules were designed to ensure that fighters competed under conditions that prioritized fairness, safety, and sportsmanship. By banning dangerous and unsportsmanlike actions, Pride aimed to protect its athletes while maintaining the integrity of the sport. Each rule in place was a reminder that MMA is not just about fighting; it's about respecting the opponent, the sport, and the audience who follow it.

Headbutting, eye gouging, and hair pulling were all actions that could cause unnecessary harm and disrupt the fairness of a fight. These moves, while they may have appeared as a quick way to gain an advantage, often led to serious injuries that could end a fighter's career prematurely. By disallowing such tactics, Pride made it clear that true warriors fought with skill, strategy, and respect, not through dirty or dangerous moves.

Similarly, rules against biting, fish hooking, and groin strikes were established to prevent the kind of chaos that could turn a fight into a spectacle of brutality. Such fouls weren't just illegal; they were an attack on the spirit of competition. Fighters who respected the rules showed that they cared more about the challenge of the sport than about winning at any cost. These fouls, when committed, didn't just harm the opponent—they harmed the sport itself.

One of the most critical fouls in Pride was targeting the back of the head. This part of the body is particularly vulnerable to severe injury, including concussions and even spinal damage. By disallowing punches to this area, Pride demonstrated a deep understanding of the physical dangers of MMA and reinforced its commitment to fighter safety. This rule was a direct response to the potential for long-term health issues, protecting fighters both in the ring and after they left it.

The prohibition of illegal actions such as throwing a fighter out of the ring or running from the fight also played a major role in maintaining order. These actions weren't just dangerous; they disrupted the flow of the match and frustrated fans who were looking for clean, intense bouts. The rules around the ropes were also important, as they kept the fighters focused on the battle within the ring, not on trying to manipulate their environment for an advantage.

The safety of fighters was especially emphasized in the event of injury. When a fighter was hurt due to an illegal action, the decision to pause the fight and give time for recovery was made with their health in mind. It was important for the match to continue only if the injured fighter was able to safely participate. If not, the offending fighter could be disqualified, sending a message that there would be consequences for reckless actions.

Pride's rules set the stage for a sport that could showcase raw talent, power, and technique without allowing the brutality to cross the line into unnecessary harm. These regulations allowed fighters to show their true skills, knowing that the playing field was leveled and that their safety was taken seriously. The respect for these rules helped elevate Pride as a premier organization in the world of MMA, showing that the sport could be both exciting and responsible.

In the end, Pride's commitment to fairness and safety helped shape the future of MMA. By enforcing these rules, they made sure that the fighters were respected and protected while giving fans a product that was both thrilling and responsible. The rules not only safeguarded the athletes but also ensured that every fight, whether it ended in victory or defeat, was a demonstration of the true spirit of competition.

Chapter 29: Match Conduct

In Pride Fighting Championships, the conduct of a match was closely regulated to ensure fairness, safety, and excitement. Referees played a crucial role in overseeing the action, especially when situations arose where the fighters were at risk of leaving the ring or becoming entangled in the ropes. In these cases, the referee would immediately stop the action, requiring the fighters to cease their movements. This was necessary to prevent one fighter from taking an unfair advantage due to the positioning, and the fighters would then be repositioned in the center of the ring. The goal was to maintain a level playing field and allow the match to resume with minimal disruption.

Once the fighters were repositioned in the center of the ring, the referee would ensure that they were in the same relative position to one another as before the interruption. This was done to maintain the fairness of the competition. The fighters were required to wait for the referee's instruction before continuing, ensuring that the action resumed smoothly and safely. This approach helped avoid any unnecessary delays or confusion during the match.

One of the key elements of match conduct was maintaining continuous action. To discourage inactivity or stalling, referees were authorized to issue penalty cards to fighters who failed to engage in the fight. This was a critical measure because MMA matches are about active combat, and fighters were expected to demonstrate their skills and engage with their opponent throughout the contest. If a fighter was deemed to be inactive, the referee could issue a warning card, indicating a 10% deduction from the fighter's purse. This served as an incentive for fighters to maintain a high level of activity throughout the fight.

The penalty system was designed to encourage action and discourage fighters from using evasive tactics to run down the clock. Inactive fighters were penalized for not engaging or showing enough effort, which kept the matches from becoming dull or uninteresting. The penalty cards were a clear reminder that in Pride, the expectation was that every fighter would give their best effort and stay involved in the action at all times.

These penalties not only helped keep the matches exciting, but they also maintained the integrity of the sport. Fighters who were looking to avoid engaging with their opponent, either through stalling or retreating, could no longer rely on these tactics without facing consequences. The 10% deduction from the purse served as a strong deterrent, making sure that fighters knew they would be held accountable for poor conduct in the ring.

In addition to ensuring a fast-paced fight, the conduct rules helped to maintain the safety of the fighters. By preventing stalling or excessive caution, the sport remained dynamic and kept the action moving forward. This was especially important in a sport as intense and physically demanding as MMA, where fighters needed to be focused and engaged to avoid unnecessary injuries.

Another important aspect of match conduct was the role of the referee in enforcing the rules. The referee had the authority to stop the fight if necessary, especially if a fighter was in danger or if the conduct of the fight was becoming too dangerous. This included situations like a fighter losing control, engaging in illegal actions, or becoming too hurt to continue safely. The referee was the final authority in ensuring that the fight continued in a safe and fair manner.

The rules around match conduct in Pride Fighting Championships helped create an environment where fighters were encouraged to perform at their highest level. With penalties for inactivity and clear instructions from referees, each match had a consistent rhythm and pace. Fighters knew that they would be expected to stay active, and that any violations would be met with consequences, ultimately preserving the excitement and integrity of the sport.

Mastering Match Conduct

In Pride Fighting Championships, match conduct was essential for maintaining fairness, safety, and excitement. The rules were carefully designed to ensure that each fight remained fast-paced and dynamic, while also protecting the fighters from unnecessary harm. The role of the referee was key to this system, as they were responsible for enforcing the rules and making sure the fighters followed the guidelines.

By stopping the fight when necessary, such as when fighters were in danger of falling out of the ring or becoming tangled in the ropes, the referees helped keep the match under control. This immediate intervention ensured that the fighters could reset and continue in a fair position. The decision to place them in the same relative position also helped maintain fairness and consistency, allowing the fight to continue without an unfair advantage.

Penalties for inactivity were another important aspect of Pride's match conduct rules. Fighters were expected to remain active and engaged throughout the match, and any attempts to stall or avoid action were penalized with a deduction from their purse. This discouraged any form of evasion and kept the fights exciting. Fighters had to demonstrate their skills and compete at a high level, ensuring that the audience was always engaged and that the sport remained competitive.

The introduction of penalty cards was an innovative approach to discouraging inaction. Fighters were no longer able to rest on their laurels or waste time; the 10% purse deduction was a significant consequence for those who were inactive. This system promoted the idea that MMA was a sport of constant action, where fighters were expected to keep moving and striving for victory, not merely to survive.

These conduct rules also protected the safety of the fighters. By discouraging stalling and encouraging active combat, the risk of unnecessary injuries was reduced. The emphasis on keeping the match flowing meant that fighters were constantly in motion, preventing dangerous situations that could occur when one fighter was retreating or unwilling to engage.

The referee's authority played a major role in the match conduct rules. If a fighter was hurt or the conduct of the match was not in line with the rules, the referee had the power to stop the fight. This ability ensured that any actions that could endanger the fighters' well-being were quickly addressed, whether it was from illegal moves or unintentional accidents.

By maintaining a high level of activity and quickly addressing any issues that arose, the match conduct rules kept the fights exciting, fair, and safe. The clear structure also allowed fighters to understand what was expected of them. They knew that staying active was the key to victory, and that any attempt to avoid the action would lead to penalties.

In the end, Pride's match conduct rules created an environment where fighters could showcase their skills without the fear of unnecessary interference. The system worked to enhance the viewing experience while keeping the sport safe and exciting for both the fighters and the fans. The careful balance of action, penalties, and referee intervention ensured that each fight would remain as fair and thrilling as possible.

Chapter 30: Matches Between Fighters of Different Weight Classes

Pride Fighting Championships was renowned for its willingness to host matches between fighters of vastly different sizes. These matchups were both thrilling and controversial, pushing the limits of strategy, skill, and endurance. To maintain fairness in such situations, Pride implemented special provisions, giving lighter fighters options that could level the playing field.

One of the key provisions was the ability for the lighter fighter to decide whether knees or kicks to the face would be allowed when in the "four points" position. This position, where a fighter is on hands and knees, often left fighters vulnerable. By giving the lighter competitor the choice to permit or prohibit these techniques, Pride acknowledged the potential dangers posed by the weight and strength differences.

In matches between middleweights with a weight difference of 10 kilograms (22 pounds) or more, this rule was particularly significant. A lighter middleweight fighter facing a larger opponent had the opportunity to limit certain attacks, reducing the likelihood of severe damage from a heavier adversary. This created an additional layer of strategy for both competitors.

The provision extended to matches between middleweight and heavyweight fighters, where the same weight difference threshold applied. The lighter middleweight could invoke the rule to restrict techniques that would otherwise leave them at a serious disadvantage. This rule encouraged fighters of different weight classes to accept challenges without feeling excessively at risk.

Among heavyweights, the rule adjusted to accommodate a larger weight disparity. If there was a difference of 15 kilograms (33 pounds) or more between two heavyweight fighters, the lighter participant retained the option to restrict knees or kicks in the four points position. This consideration was critical in ensuring the sport remained competitive, even when the fighters had significant size differences.

These provisions highlighted Pride's commitment to safety and fairness while embracing the unpredictability of cross-weight-class matches. The organization valued the spectacle of a smaller, skilled fighter facing off against a larger, more powerful opponent. The rules allowed the smaller fighter to compete on more even terms, preserving the integrity of the fight.

The responsibility of enforcing these provisions rested with the referees. They ensured that both fighters were aware of the rules and that the lighter fighter's choice was honored throughout the match. Any violation of the agreed-upon terms was met with warnings or penalties, emphasizing the importance of fair play.

Despite these provisions, matches between fighters of different weight classes demanded immense courage and preparation from all participants. The heavier fighter often relied on strength and power, while the lighter competitor needed speed, technique, and strategy to succeed. This dynamic made such matches unpredictable and exciting for fans.

Pride's willingness to embrace these unique matchups contributed to its legendary status in MMA history. These battles showcased the resilience, adaptability, and determination of fighters, creating unforgettable moments that still resonate with fans today. The special provisions reflected Pride's understanding of the challenges involved and its dedication to promoting thrilling, competitive, and fair fights.

The Final Bell: Balancing Strength and Skill Across Divisions

Matches between fighters of different weight classes in Pride Fighting Championships provided a unique challenge that showcased the spirit of the sport. These battles were not just about size or strength but demonstrated how rules could make the fights more balanced and strategic. The special provisions for lighter fighters ensured that even in seemingly uneven matchups, skill and strategy played a significant role.

The option for lighter fighters to limit certain techniques, like knees and kicks to the face in the four points position, was a crucial element of this balance. It allowed them to enter the ring with a measure of protection against the overwhelming power of heavier opponents. These rules recognized the dangers of weight disparities while preserving the excitement of cross-weight matchups.

By allowing these adjustments, Pride encouraged fighters to take on challenges that might have otherwise seemed impossible. It wasn't just about survival—it was about creating opportunities for lighter fighters to outmaneuver their larger opponents through creativity and precision. This approach highlighted the artistry and adaptability required in mixed martial arts.

Fans were captivated by the unpredictability of these matches. A lighter fighter often brought speed, agility, and technical expertise to the ring, while the heavier competitor relied on raw power and durability. The result was an intense clash of contrasting styles, making each fight a thrilling spectacle.

The provisions also reflected Pride's respect for the fighters' safety and well-being. Balancing the excitement of the sport with precautions against serious harm ensured that these matches were not only entertaining but also responsibly managed. This combination of care and competition cemented Pride's reputation as a leader in MMA.

For referees, enforcing these rules added complexity to their role. They had to ensure that the lighter fighter's choices were respected and that the rules were followed strictly. Their diligence helped maintain the integrity of the matches and reinforced Pride's commitment to fairness.

These matches celebrated the essence of martial arts— where technique and determination could overcome size and strength. Fighters who triumphed in these battles became legends, remembered for their courage and skill in taking on daunting challenges. Their victories inspired fans and competitors alike.

Through these special rules, Pride transformed weight class mismatches into opportunities for innovation and excitement. These fights reminded everyone why MMA is a sport that values both power and precision, making it a spectacle that continues to inspire and amaze fans around the world.

Chapter 31: Pride Bushido

Pride Bushido was a unique series of events within the Pride Fighting Championships, offering a distinct flavor compared to the main Pride events. The name "Bushido" means "the way of the warrior" in Japanese, referring to the principles and moral code followed by samurai. These events embodied that spirit, showcasing bravery, skill, and innovation. Bushido provided opportunities for experimental fight formats, allowing country-versus-country or team-versus-team competitions. It also served as a proving ground for rising fighters, giving them a platform to shine through "Challenge Matches" that followed special rules.

One key difference in Pride Bushido events was the fight duration. Regular bouts consisted of two rounds—the first lasting ten minutes and the second lasting five—with two-minute intermissions. These slightly shorter matches required fighters to strategize differently, focusing on explosive performances from the outset. Challenge Matches, however, consisted of two five-minute rounds, giving even newer competitors a chance to showcase their abilities without the physical strain of longer matches.

Red cards added another layer of uniqueness to Bushido events. Similar to yellow cards in Pride FC, a red card penalized fighters who stalled or avoided offense, deducting 10% of their fight purse. Unlike yellow cards, red cards could be issued without limit and did not result in disqualification. This approach discouraged inactivity, pushing fighters to keep the action moving. Officials were particularly strict in enforcing rules against holding for stalemates or failing to make genuine attempts to finish the match.

The team competitions in Bushido stood out as a fan favorite. These events emphasized national pride and camaraderie, with fighters representing their countries or teams in spirited battles. This format allowed viewers to rally behind their favorite nations or groups, creating an electric atmosphere. Fighters on these teams also gained valuable experience, working together to develop strategies that played to their collective strengths.

Bushido's experimental nature also opened doors for fighters who might not have fit into the traditional Pride FC mold. Rising stars and lesser-known fighters were given the chance to prove their mettle against tough opponents, earning recognition in a highly competitive environment. For many, a standout performance in Bushido became a springboard to main Pride events or international MMA stardom.

The Challenge Matches added an exciting element to Bushido, pitting fighters against one another under conditions designed to highlight their technical abilities. These matches encouraged creativity and adaptability, as fighters had to adjust to rules that differed slightly from what they might have been used to. This innovation kept the Bushido series fresh and unpredictable.

The combination of shorter matches, stricter rules, and team dynamics made Pride Bushido a fascinating chapter in the history of MMA. It allowed Pride to experiment with formats and ideas that expanded the sport's appeal, drawing in both hardcore fans and newcomers. These events celebrated the essence of martial arts—the pursuit of excellence and the warrior spirit.

Bushido wasn't just a sideline to the main Pride FC events; it was an integral part of Pride's legacy. It pushed fighters to adapt, innovate, and bring their best to the ring, leaving fans with unforgettable moments. The way of the warrior lived on through these events, making Bushido a cornerstone of Pride Fighting Championships.

The Spirit of Bushido Lives On

Pride Bushido wasn't just a series of fights; it was a celebration of the martial arts spirit, innovation, and international camaraderie. These events gave MMA fans a unique experience, showcasing a blend of fast-paced action, experimental formats, and opportunities for emerging talent. By offering something different from the main Pride FC events, Bushido created its own identity and carved out a special place in the sport's history.

The red card system, exclusive to Bushido, emphasized constant action. Fighters had to push forward, avoiding stalling or any strategy that led to a stalemate. This rule ensured matches stayed dynamic and exciting for the audience, while also rewarding fighters who embodied the true spirit of competition. Unlike other penalties, the red card didn't lead to disqualification, which allowed for a greater focus on action over rigid outcomes.

Shorter bouts in Bushido demanded strategic precision and stamina. Fighters couldn't afford to take their time or pace themselves too cautiously. Every moment in the ring counted, with fewer rounds and less time to impress the judges or secure a victory. This high-pressure format favored fighters who could adapt quickly and perform under intense conditions.

Team competitions added a layer of pride and unity to the events. Whether representing their country or a collective fight camp, these team-based battles brought fighters and fans together, celebrating the diversity of talent and styles in MMA. The national pride on display during these matches added emotional weight, making victories and defeats even more impactful.

Bushido also gave newer or less-established fighters a rare chance to prove themselves. By introducing Challenge Matches, Pride allowed these athletes to step into the spotlight and showcase their skills under modified rules. For many fighters, this was a stepping stone to larger stages, providing invaluable experience against tough opponents.

The name "Bushido" was more than a title; it reflected the very essence of these events. Fighters embodied the samurai's values of courage, discipline, and respect, bringing martial arts' philosophical roots to the forefront. Bushido served as a reminder that MMA isn't just about winning but about competing with honor and pushing one's limits.

Pride Bushido's innovative approach to fight cards and rule sets left an enduring mark on MMA. These events showed that the sport could evolve and grow while staying true to its core principles. Fighters who succeeded in Bushido demonstrated not just skill but adaptability, paving the way for future stars and trends in the sport.

As we look back on Pride Bushido, it's clear that these events weren't just about the fights themselves—they were about the bigger picture. Bushido pushed the boundaries of MMA, created unforgettable moments, and reminded everyone of the deep traditions that underlie the sport. The spirit of the warrior, captured so perfectly in these events, continues to inspire fighters and fans alike.

Chapter 32: Differences from the Unified Rules of Mixed Martial Arts

Pride Fighting Championships distinguished itself through its unique set of rules, which contrasted significantly with the Unified Rules of Mixed Martial Arts (MMA). These differences played a vital role in defining Pride's identity and style, shaping a distinct experience for fighters and fans alike. While the Unified Rules aimed for uniformity and safety, Pride's rules allowed for a more aggressive and dynamic style of competition.

One of the most notable differences was Pride's allowance of kicks and knees to the head of a downed opponent. Under Unified Rules, this is strictly prohibited and considered a foul. Pride's approach encouraged fighters to maintain control and awareness even when on the ground, making ground positions more dynamic and dangerous.

Stomping the head of a downed opponent was another allowance in Pride that contrasted sharply with the Unified Rules, where such actions are prohibited. These stomps became an iconic aspect of Pride fights, creating moments of high drama and showcasing the brutality of the sport. They also required fighters to develop defensive techniques specifically to counter such moves.

Pride permitted the use of piledrivers—spiking an opponent onto the canvas head or neck first—a move considered a foul under Unified Rules. While controversial, this added another layer of strategy and excitement to grappling exchanges in Pride matches.

Interestingly, Pride prohibited elbow strikes to the head of an opponent, even though the Unified Rules allowed them with certain restrictions, such as banning strikes that move directly downward (12 to 6 o'clock). This ban in Pride aimed to reduce the likelihood of cuts, which could prematurely end fights and frustrate both fighters and fans.

Another major difference lay in the fight format. Pride used a ten-minute first round, followed by shorter rounds, with two-minute rest periods. This longer initial round allowed fighters to develop strategies, work for submissions, and showcase their skills without the immediate pressure of the shorter five-minute rounds mandated by the Unified Rules.

Judging criteria also varied significantly. Pride judged the fight as a whole rather than scoring each round individually, as done under the ten-point must system in the Unified Rules. This approach gave judges a broader perspective, encouraging fighters to focus on the overall impact and effort throughout the fight rather than narrowly winning individual rounds.

The March 2007 announcement that Pride would transition to Unified Rules brought mixed reactions. This shift meant losing elements like stomps, ground knees, and the ten-minute first round—rules that had defined Pride's uniqueness. However, the change never materialized in future events, as Pride ceased operations after Pride 34.

The differences between Pride and the Unified Rules remain a fascinating chapter in MMA history. They reflect not just different priorities—entertainment versus uniformity—but also the evolution of the sport. Pride's rules created a legacy of legendary moments, influencing fighters and promotions even after its closure. For many fans, Pride's approach to MMA remains unmatched in its intensity and spectacle.

The Legacy of Pride's Ruleset

Pride's unique ruleset, different from the Unified Rules of Mixed Martial Arts, has left an indelible mark on the sport, remembered for its intensity and innovation. These rules shaped the way fighters prepared and competed, creating unforgettable moments in MMA history.

The decision to allow moves such as stomps, kicks to a grounded opponent, and even piledrivers created a sense of danger and excitement. These techniques required fighters to approach every second of a match with heightened awareness, knowing that any lapse in defense could result in a devastating attack. It wasn't just about skill—it was about survival and adaptability.

The long ten-minute opening rounds added depth to Pride fights. Fighters were granted more time to execute strategies, seek submissions, and adapt to their opponents. This contrasted with the rapid pace of five-minute rounds under the Unified Rules, emphasizing endurance and creative problem-solving during extended exchanges.

Judging the fight as a whole, rather than round-by-round, provided a broader evaluation of a fighter's performance. It encouraged sustained effort, with fighters knowing that an early mistake could still be overshadowed by a dominant finish. This scoring system pushed competitors to showcase their skills throughout the match rather than relying on narrow victories in individual rounds.

Pride's refusal to allow elbows to the head may have minimized superficial injuries like cuts but ensured fights weren't prematurely halted. This decision reflected the promotion's priority for continuous action and fair outcomes, allowing matches to progress without unnecessary interruptions.

The incorporation of elements like red and yellow cards to penalize inactivity added a level of accountability. Fighters were pushed to remain aggressive and engage actively, reducing stalling and ensuring fans were consistently entertained. This approach resonated with audiences craving high-energy and high-stakes battles.

When Pride was set to transition to the Unified Rules in 2007, it marked the end of an era. While these changes aimed for standardization, they symbolized a departure from the raw, unfiltered style that had come to define Pride. Even though these rules were never implemented, the prospect alone sparked debates about balancing fighter safety with the essence of the sport.

Pride's ruleset remains a cherished memory for MMA enthusiasts. It was a system that demanded bravery, skill, and creativity from its fighters. Though the organization has been gone for years, its legacy endures in the hearts of fans and fighters alike, proving that its spirit was truly one of a kind.

Part Seven: The Spectacle of Pride Events

Chapter 33: The Legacy of Pride Events

Pride events began with grandeur, highlighted by the iconic theme music PRIDE, composed by Yasuharu Takanashi. This electrifying anthem set the tone for the evening, blending excitement and anticipation. Each match concluded with Victory, another masterpiece by Takanashi, capturing the triumph of the winners and the unforgettable moments of the night. These musical choices helped elevate the production value, making Pride events feel more like theatrical spectacles than just combat sports.

Pride's "numbered" events were the main attraction, showcasing the world's best fighters in highly anticipated matchups. These events were known for their scale, often hosted in massive venues with thousands of fans. However, Pride also introduced specialized event series to cater to different formats and fighter showcases. For instance, Pride: Bushido served as a platform for rising stars and unique team-based competitions. It allowed fans to witness a variety of matchups while fighters gained valuable experience in the spotlight.

Another notable series was the Pride Grand Prix, a tournament-style event that highlighted the skill and endurance of competitors. Fighters had to win multiple bouts in a single night to advance, creating some of the most dramatic and grueling moments in Pride history. These events were designed to determine the best of the best, often culminating in legendary showdowns that etched themselves into MMA lore.

Pride also hosted Shockwave, a special crossover event that combined MMA with professional wrestling elements. These events were especially popular in Japan, bridging the gap between two passionate fanbases. Fighters and performers alike embraced the unique atmosphere, making Shockwave an annual highlight for many fans.

Another innovation was the Pride New Year's Eve shows, which became iconic celebrations blending martial arts and entertainment. These events often featured special rules, celebrity appearances, and extraordinary matchups. They exemplified Pride's willingness to experiment, making them a cultural phenomenon beyond the sport itself.

The production of Pride events was unmatched, with dramatic entrances, elaborate pyrotechnics, and theatrical lighting. Fighters walked out to personalized music, adding to their mystique and individuality. The blend of sportsmanship, drama, and storytelling made every event feel larger than life, resonating deeply with fans.

Commentary played a vital role in enhancing the viewer experience. Pride's English broadcasts featured a mix of passionate analysts who brought the action to life for international audiences. Meanwhile, Japanese commentary captured the cultural nuances and fervor of the sport, making the events universally appealing.

Pride's events were not just competitions; they were experiences that transcended the cage. They united fans worldwide, from the arenas in Japan to living rooms across the globe. By blending martial arts, entertainment, and cultural elements, Pride created a legacy that continues to influence MMA promotions today.

The combination of music, grand production, diverse event series, and unforgettable matchups solidified Pride's place as a trailblazer in combat sports. Its events remain celebrated, not only for their fights but for the spectacle they delivered, leaving an enduring mark on the world of MMA.

Beyond the Fights: The Magic of Pride Events

Pride Fighting Championships events were more than just a series of matches; they were a celebration of combat, culture, and entertainment. From the moment the first note of PRIDE theme music played, the atmosphere was electric. The deliberate choice of music like PRIDE and Victory reflected not only the technical excellence of Yasuharu Takanashi's compositions but also Pride's commitment to creating a complete sensory experience for fans. These moments framed the events, offering a grand opening and a triumphant conclusion to each fight, leaving audiences emotionally charged.

Pride's events were monumental in scale and ambition, making every numbered event feel like a must-watch occasion. The detailed production and massive arenas added to the allure, emphasizing the grandeur that Pride sought to deliver. Fans were not just attending an MMA event; they were stepping into a world where combat became an art form, and fighters were elevated to the status of warriors.

What set Pride apart was its creativity in diversifying event formats. Pride: Bushido brought something fresh, offering opportunities for rising stars and unique match structures like team-based competitions. This flexibility gave new talent a chance to shine while maintaining the excitement for seasoned fans. The Bushido events were proof of Pride's ability to innovate without losing the essence of the sport.

The Grand Prix tournaments, in particular, captured the spirit of competition in its rawest form. Fighters needed not only skill but incredible endurance to succeed. Fans witnessed extraordinary feats of strength and determination as competitors battled through multiple matches in a single night. These tournaments became a hallmark of Pride, etching unforgettable moments into the history of MMA.

Shockwave and New Year's Eve shows were examples of Pride's ability to think outside the box. By blending MMA with pro wrestling or introducing elements of spectacle and celebration, Pride created events that appealed to a broader audience. These shows demonstrated that combat sports could be entertaining without sacrificing authenticity.

The meticulous attention to production details, from dramatic fighter entrances to the lighting and pyrotechnics, set Pride apart. Every aspect was designed to create an immersive experience that lingered in fans' memories long after the event ended. Fighters became larger-than-life characters, each entrance and match amplifying their individual stories.

Commentary and storytelling added depth to the action, with analysts providing context that resonated with both seasoned viewers and newcomers. This mix of technical insight and passion helped make the events accessible to fans worldwide. Pride mastered the balance of local flair and global appeal, ensuring its legacy reached far beyond Japan.

Ultimately, Pride events went beyond the sport itself. They united fans in a shared experience, transcending cultural and language barriers. The combination of artistry, strategy, and sheer spectacle created an atmosphere unmatched in combat sports. This legacy endures, influencing how MMA is celebrated and reminding fans of the heights the sport can achieve when innovation and tradition merge.

Chapter 34: Pride Grand Prix

The Pride Grand Prix tournaments were among the most prestigious events in mixed martial arts history. These tournaments brought together the best fighters in the world to compete for the title of champion and a significant monetary prize. While the winner was awarded a championship belt, it was symbolic of their victory in the tournament and not a title that would be defended in subsequent matches. These events showcased the highest level of competition and became a platform for legends to be born.

Pride's first Grand Prix was held in 2000 and had no weight limits, making it an openweight competition. This inaugural tournament unfolded over two events. The opening round determined the fighters who would advance, while the finals featured quarter-finals, semi-finals, and the ultimate championship bout. This openweight format highlighted the diversity of fighters and strategies, making it an unforgettable start to Pride's tournament legacy.

In 2003, Pride introduced a middleweight Grand Prix, shifting focus to specific weight classes. This tournament was spread across two events: *Total Elimination 2003*, which featured first-round bouts, and *Final Conflict 2003*, which hosted the semi-finals and final. This format became the blueprint for future tournaments, providing fans with a clear progression and maintaining excitement over multiple events.

By 2004, the tournament structure expanded to include three stages: *Total Elimination*, *Critical Countdown*, and *Final Conflict*. These events combined tournament bouts with non-tournament matches, ensuring that every card was packed with thrilling action. This approach balanced showcasing Grand Prix contenders and keeping fans engaged with other highly anticipated fights.

One of the most unique moments in Grand Prix history occurred during the 2000 Finals. The match between Kazushi Sakuraba and Royce Gracie was held under special rules requested by Gracie, with no time limit and no judges. The contest lasted an astonishing 90 minutes, ending when Gracie's corner threw in the towel due to his injuries. This grueling match highlighted the endurance and willpower required to succeed in such a demanding tournament.

In 2005, Pride crowned its first welterweight and lightweight champions during the Shockwave event, adding even more significance to that year's Grand Prix tournaments. Fighters like Dan Henderson and Takanori Gomi cemented their legacies by winning these inaugural titles, showcasing the depth of talent in these lighter weight classes.

The 2006 Openweight Grand Prix was another historic event, featuring legendary fighters from different divisions. Mirko "Cro Cop" Filipović emerged victorious, proving that skill and determination could overcome size and weight differences. This tournament reinforced the idea that Grand Prix events were not just about physical attributes but also about strategy and heart.

By 2007, Pride planned to host one Grand Prix annually, rotating between the four established weight classes. While this approach aimed to streamline the tournaments and maintain their prestige, Pride's eventual acquisition by the UFC meant that these plans never fully materialized. Nonetheless, the Grand

Prix events remain a cornerstone of Pride's legacy, celebrated by fans for their excitement, unpredictability, and unforgettable moments.

Pride Grand Prix tournaments were more than competitions; they were a spectacle that united fans worldwide. From the openweight battles to the strategic brilliance of weight-class-specific events, these tournaments showcased the essence of mixed martial arts and solidified Pride's place in the history of the sport.

The Legacy of Grand Prix Glory

The Pride Grand Prix tournaments were a true celebration of martial arts excellence. They brought together some of the best fighters in the world, showcasing skill, heart, and determination. These tournaments tested not just physical strength but also the mental fortitude of every competitor. Winning a Grand Prix was more than just a victory—it was a moment of immortality in the sport's history.

Each Grand Prix was unique, offering fans thrilling stories and unforgettable moments. From Mark Coleman's dominance in 2000 to Wanderlei Silva's middleweight reign in 2003, the tournaments consistently raised the bar for competition. Fighters like Fedor Emelianenko, Mirko Cro Cop, and Takanori Gomi carved their names into history, creating legacies that are still celebrated today.

The Grand Prix format pushed fighters to their limits. Competing multiple times in one night demanded peak conditioning and resilience. It wasn't just about defeating a single opponent—it was about conquering the entire field of elite contenders. For fans, this format provided endless excitement and unpredictability, with every fight holding the potential for upsets and unforgettable finishes.

The tournaments also highlighted the diversity of styles in mixed martial arts. Wrestlers, strikers, and submission specialists all had their moments to shine. This mix of styles made every match a clash of strategies, where preparation and adaptability were as crucial as raw power. Pride's willingness to embrace this diversity set it apart from other promotions.

Pride Grand Prix events were more than just competitions—they were spectacles. The pageantry, the roaring crowds, and the electric atmosphere made every event feel like a cultural phenomenon. Fans across the globe tuned in, united by their love of martial arts and the drama of the tournaments.

The 2005 Shockwave event, crowning both welterweight and lightweight champions, was a turning point, blending tournament glory with championship stakes. It showcased Pride's ability to innovate and adapt, keeping the sport fresh and exciting for its audience.

While the tournaments were demanding, they also rewarded perseverance. Fighters who triumphed earned not only financial rewards but also the respect of their peers and adoration of fans. The Pride Grand Prix winners became icons, their names synonymous with the spirit of competition.

The legacy of the Pride Grand Prix lives on in the memories of fans and the careers it shaped. These tournaments captured the essence of martial arts—the pursuit of excellence, the thrill of competition, and the unyielding spirit of warriors. Even today, the stories of these legendary events inspire fighters and fans alike, reminding everyone why the Grand Prix was truly special.

Chapter 35: Pride Bushido

Pride Bushido was introduced in 2003 as a unique series focused on lighter fighters, providing a platform that allowed these athletes to shine. Unlike Pride's main events, which often emphasized heavyweight competitors, Bushido was designed to showcase the skill, speed, and technique of fighters in the lightweight (73 kg) and welterweight (83 kg) divisions. It filled an important gap in the organization, offering fans a different flavor of mixed martial arts action.

The first Pride Bushido event set the tone for what would become a beloved series. Fighters in these weight classes were known for their speed and precision, and Bushido brought their talents into the spotlight. The events were fast-paced and often featured back-to-back exciting matches, earning the series a loyal following. These lighter competitors demonstrated that size wasn't the only determinant of greatness in martial arts.

Bushido wasn't just about smaller weight classes. It also experimented with unique formats and styles of competition. In addition to single fights, Bushido incorporated team competitions and country-versus-country events. These formats created a sense of camaraderie and pride, as fighters battled not just for themselves but for their teams or nations.

In 2005, Pride Bushido introduced its own lightweight and welterweight Grand Prix tournaments. These tournaments were a game-changer, putting an official stamp of prestige on the lighter divisions. Starting with eight-man brackets, the tournaments featured elite fighters competing in quarter-finals and semi-finals at Pride Bushido 9. The finals were held at the legendary Pride Shockwave 2005 event. Winning a Grand Prix was no easy feat, but those who did were crowned as champions and elevated to the status of stars within the organization.

The Bushido series wasn't limited to just tournaments. It also served as a proving ground for rising talent. Many fighters who started in Bushido would later go on to compete in Pride's main events, establishing themselves as household names in mixed martial arts. The series allowed Pride to build a deep roster of talent across all weight classes, enhancing the overall quality of their shows.

By the time Bushido 13 concluded, the series had become an integral part of Pride's identity. However, it was announced that the series would come to an end, with its weight classes being absorbed into the main Pride shows. While this marked the conclusion of Bushido as a standalone series, its influence was felt long after. The fighters who emerged from Bushido continued to shape the future of the sport, both in Pride and in other organizations.

Bushido's emphasis on skill, speed, and strategy left a lasting impact on fans and fighters alike. It demonstrated that lighter fighters could deliver just as much excitement and drama as their heavier counterparts. The series pushed the boundaries of what was possible in mixed martial arts, setting a standard for how lighter divisions should be showcased.

Pride Bushido will always be remembered as a groundbreaking series that gave a platform to a new generation of fighters. It celebrated diversity in the sport and proved that martial arts isn't just about power but also about precision, heart, and technique. The legacy of Bushido lives on in the stories of its fighters and the fans who cherished every moment of its unforgettable matches.

A Legacy of Lightweights: The Impact of Bushido

Pride Bushido wasn't just a series of events; it was a transformative force in mixed martial arts. It carved out a space for lighter fighters to showcase their skills, proving that speed, technique, and strategy could rival the raw power seen in heavyweight divisions. This chapter of Pride's history left an indelible mark on the sport and its fans.

Bushido events created a new identity within Pride, delivering a unique atmosphere that set them apart from the main shows. The emphasis on fast-paced action and technical battles gave fans something fresh to enjoy. Fighters in the lightweight and welterweight divisions seized this opportunity to demonstrate that they could steal the show just as effectively as their heavier peers.

The tournaments held under the Bushido banner were defining moments. These Grand Prix competitions brought global attention to the talent in the lighter weight classes. Winning a Bushido tournament was more than just earning a belt; it was a statement of excellence and a gateway to superstardom. Fighters like Takanori Gomi and Dan Henderson emerged as legends, with Bushido playing a pivotal role in their careers.

Bushido was more than just individual glory. The team and country-versus-country formats added a layer of pride and rivalry that electrified audiences. These matches brought fighters together in unique ways, showcasing the diverse styles and approaches of martial artists from around the world.

The end of Bushido as a standalone series marked a turning point, but its influence continued. By integrating lightweight and welterweight fighters into the main Pride shows, the organization ensured that the skills and energy of these competitors would never be overlooked. The decision highlighted the growing importance of these divisions in the broader MMA landscape.

For fans, Bushido was a reminder of the beauty of martial arts in all its forms. It was a celebration of discipline, creativity, and the human spirit. Each event told stories of underdogs, rising stars, and epic battles, leaving lasting memories for those who witnessed them.

Bushido also inspired future MMA organizations to invest in showcasing lighter weight classes. The series proved that smaller fighters could deliver big moments, helping to shape the evolution of the sport on a global scale.

Looking back, Pride Bushido stands as a symbol of innovation and inclusivity in mixed martial arts. It wasn't just a series; it was a movement that championed diversity in fighting styles, weight classes, and competition formats. Its legacy lives on in the fighters it launched, the fans it inspired, and the standards it set for the sport.

Chapter 36: Pride The Best

Pride launched *The Best* in 2002 as an experimental series aimed at highlighting up-and-coming fighters. This was an opportunity for less experienced athletes to prove themselves on a big stage, surrounded by the prestige of the Pride brand. Unlike the main Pride events, which focused on seasoned professionals and established stars, *The Best* offered fresh faces a platform to showcase their potential.

The ring used for *The Best* was unique compared to traditional Pride events. Instead of the usual square ring, the series featured an eight-sided roped ring. This design provided fighters with a distinct competitive environment, emphasizing agility and adaptability. Fans appreciated the change, as it added an element of unpredictability to the matches and set the events apart from Pride's other offerings.

The format of *The Best* also allowed for more experimental matchups. Fighters from various disciplines were given opportunities to test their skills against opponents with diverse fighting styles. This mix of talent and technique helped create memorable moments for fans and valuable experiences for the fighters involved.

Despite its potential, *The Best* faced challenges. After just three shows, the series was discontinued in October 2002. Factors like scheduling conflicts, financial considerations, and the overwhelming popularity of Pride's main events likely contributed to this decision. While short-lived, the series had planted seeds for future innovations in Pride's event structure.

The concept behind *The Best* did not go to waste. Elements of the series were refined and incorporated into Pride Bushido, which debuted in 2003. By shifting the focus to lighter weight classes and introducing new formats like team competitions, Bushido carried forward the spirit of *The Best* while reaching broader audiences.

For the fighters who participated in *The Best*, the experience was invaluable. Many of them went on to compete in Pride's main events, using the skills and confidence they gained during their time in the series. Even after its discontinuation, the legacy of *The Best* could be seen in the careers it helped launch.

Fans who attended *The Best* events fondly remember the energy and enthusiasm that surrounded these shows. The series gave them a glimpse of the next generation of talent, ensuring that Pride's future remained exciting and unpredictable.

While *The Best* may not have lasted long, it was an important chapter in Pride's history. It demonstrated the organization's willingness to take risks and explore new ideas, even if they didn't always work out as planned. The lessons learned from *The Best* ultimately strengthened Pride, paving the way for its later successes and cementing its place in MMA history.

The Legacy of Pride The Best

Pride The Best was a bold experiment that briefly expanded the scope of mixed martial arts. Although it lasted only a short time, from 2002 until the end of that year, the series provided a unique opportunity for emerging fighters to compete under the Pride banner.

Its main goal was to showcase fighters who hadn't yet made a name for themselves in the main events, offering them the chance to gain exposure and test their skills against new competition. This innovation helped Pride position itself as an organization that was open to new ideas and willing to take risks, which was crucial in growing the sport of MMA during that time.

The use of the eight-sided roped ring made these events distinctive, setting them apart from the usual Pride events that utilized the traditional ring. While the traditional square format worked well for more experienced fighters, the octagon-like ring required more agility, pushing fighters to adapt to the unique dynamics of their surroundings. This change allowed fans to see a different type of fight and gave the competitors a different kind of challenge. It proved that even minor adjustments could make a major difference in how the sport was perceived and experienced.

Despite the changes, *The Best* faced several challenges that led to its eventual discontinuation. While the idea was compelling, logistical issues, the financial demands of running additional events, and the overwhelming popularity of Pride's main tournaments likely contributed to the series' premature end. However, in its brief time, the series was able to gather a loyal fan base, providing a glimpse into the future of MMA.

The cancellation of *The Best* did not mark the end of its influence. Elements of the series' structure were carried over into Pride Bushido, a series that would further focus on lighter weight classes and introduce more experimental fight formats. Pride Bushido

194

provided another platform for up-and-coming fighters, continuing the spirit of *The Best* but on a larger and more refined scale.

In terms of career progression, *The Best* proved to be a stepping stone for many fighters. Even though it was short-lived, it gave fighters valuable experience in the spotlight of a major MMA promotion. Some of these fighters later rose to prominence in Pride's more prestigious events, and their time in *The Best* helped them build the skills and confidence they needed for future success.

The fans who were fortunate enough to witness *The Best* events fondly remember the excitement that surrounded them. It was a time when the sport was still growing, and each new event felt fresh and unpredictable. While *The Best* didn't achieve the same long-term recognition as Pride's main shows or Grand Prix tournaments, it contributed to the overall growth of MMA and the Pride brand.

Looking back, it's clear that *The Best* was a valuable experiment that helped shape Pride's evolution. It highlighted the organization's commitment to fostering new talent and expanding the reach of MMA. While it didn't last long, its influence is still felt today in the way MMA promotions give younger fighters the opportunity to develop their skills in front of large audiences.

Pride The Best was a short-lived but significant part of Pride's history. Its unique format and emphasis on new talent contributed to the legacy of Pride as an innovative force in mixed martial arts. Even though the series didn't have a long run, its spirit of exploration and risk-taking paved the way for future events that continue to shape the sport today.

Chapter 37: Final Champions

The history of Pride FC is filled with fierce competition, and its final champions represent the pinnacle of the organization's achievements. As the promotion drew to a close, several fighters held titles in different weight divisions, showcasing their dominance in the sport. However, when Zuffa LLC purchased Pride FC, the company moved to unify the Pride titles with their own UFC belts. This process marked the beginning of the end for Pride's reign in the MMA world.

Pride's heavyweight division saw Russia's Fedor Emelianenko rise to prominence, holding the title from March 2003. Emelianenko's reign was one of the longest and most dominant in MMA history. Known for his versatility and technical ability, he defended his title three times, solidifying his place as one of the greatest heavyweights of all time. Fedor's accomplishments in Pride helped elevate the organization to international recognition and left a lasting legacy.

In the middleweight division, Dan Henderson was the champion heading into Pride's final days. He had earned the title on February 24, 2007, after defeating Wanderlei Silva, but his reign was short-lived. As Pride was bought out by Zuffa, Henderson found himself in two unification bouts. In September 2007, he lost to Quinton "Rampage" Jackson, and in March 2008, Anderson Silva defeated him, marking the end of his brief reign as Pride's middleweight champion.

Dan Henderson also held the welterweight title, which he won on December 31, 2005. Like his middleweight title, his reign was cut short when the UFC took over and the titles were unified. Henderson's time in Pride marked the peak of his career, as he held both the middleweight and welterweight titles simultaneously. Though he didn't defend the welterweight belt before the Zuffa takeover, his legacy as a champion in Pride is undeniable.

The lightweight division was headed by Japan's Takanori Gomi, who captured the title on December 31, 2005. Known as "The Fireball Kid," Gomi was a fan favorite for his aggressive style and explosive striking. He defended the lightweight title once during his reign, cementing his place as one of Japan's most celebrated fighters. His success in Pride made him a standout in the lightweight category and helped elevate the sport in his home country.

The final champions of Pride represent a diverse group of fighters who each brought something unique to the sport. Their skills and accomplishments were a testament to the high level of competition that Pride fostered throughout its history. Each fighter who held a title in Pride left their mark on the organization, whether through incredible victories, memorable defenses, or dominance in their respective weight classes.

As Pride transitioned to the UFC, the champions who held titles at the time found themselves facing new challenges under the unified rules of MMA. Fighters like Henderson and Gomi continued their careers in the UFC, while Fedor Emelianenko remained one of the top heavyweights in the world, although he never fought in the UFC. The legacy of Pride's champions continues to be felt in MMA today.

Pride's final champions were among the best in the history of mixed martial arts. Their reigns were marked by incredible battles, dominant performances, and unforgettable moments. Even after the organization's closure, their achievements in Pride continue to shape the future of the sport. Through their efforts, they helped Pride secure its place as one of the most influential MMA promotions of all time.

The Legacy of Pride's Final Champions

Pride FC's history was defined by thrilling bouts, intense rivalries, and extraordinary athletes who made lasting impacts on the world of mixed martial arts. As the organization came to an end, its final champions represented the peak of Pride's era. These fighters became icons, not just for their ability to compete at the highest level but for their contributions to the sport's growth and global popularity. The final champions, including Fedor Emelianenko, Dan Henderson, Takanori Gomi, and others, helped cement Pride's place as a legendary promotion in the MMA world.

Fedor Emelianenko, the heavyweight champion, is perhaps the most iconic of them all. His dominance from March 2003 onwards was unmatched, with a fighting style that was both technically precise and deceptively simple. Fedor's three title defenses showcased his exceptional ability to adapt, remain calm under pressure, and outclass his opponents. He was widely regarded as the best heavyweight fighter during his time in Pride, and his success played a huge role in elevating the organization to a global audience.

In the middleweight division, Dan Henderson was a standout champion. His reign, which began in

February 2007, may have been brief, but it was impactful. Henderson's loss to Quinton "Rampage" Jackson in the unification bout marked the end of Pride's middleweight era, but his accomplishments in Pride still made him a respected figure in the sport. Henderson's dual reign as both the welterweight and middleweight champion helped cement his legacy as one of the most versatile and accomplished fighters in MMA history.

Similarly, Dan Henderson's welterweight reign was notable, despite not defending the title before the unification process. Henderson's dual championship status in both weight classes made him a powerful figure in Pride and added to the mystique of the organization. His championship reigns were a testament to his versatility as a fighter and his ability to succeed in multiple divisions.

Takanori Gomi, known as "The Fireball Kid," became the lightweight champion in 2005. His powerful striking and relentless aggression in the octagon made him a fan favorite and a feared competitor. Gomi's reign as lightweight champion, though short, was significant. He brought attention to the lightweight division, and his single title defense cemented his place as one of the best to have ever competed in Pride. He helped lay the groundwork for the future of lighter weight classes in MMA, proving that lighter fighters could capture the same level of excitement and attention as heavier fighters.

Pride's champions were not just fighters—they were symbols of excellence and skill. Their victories, whether in brutal knockout performances or gritty submissions, left a lasting legacy. These champions inspired future generations of fighters, proving that it's not just about strength or size but technique, heart, and determination.

As the organization transitioned to the UFC, these champions found themselves facing new challenges in a different arena. The unification of titles meant that the fighters who held Pride's belts had to adjust to new rules, new competition, and the intense spotlight of the UFC. While some continued to dominate, like Fedor Emelianenko in other promotions, others like Dan Henderson found themselves in tough battles with new champions like Quinton "Rampage" Jackson and Anderson Silva.

The champions who held titles in Pride's final years helped shape the MMA world as we know it today. Their rivalries, title defenses, and unique fighting styles set the standard for future competitions. Pride's final champions weren't just the best of their time — they were instrumental in transforming MMA into a mainstream global sport. Their achievements remain a testament to Pride's legacy, which continues to influence the sport even after the promotion's closure.

Ultimately, the final champions of Pride were more than just athletes. They were ambassadors for the sport, representing the values and culture of MMA to a global audience. Their skill, dedication, and heart remain a part of MMA's rich history, and the mark they left on the sport will never be forgotten. The champions of Pride, particularly those who held titles in the organization's final days, will forever be remembered as some of the greatest fighters to ever grace the sport of mixed martial arts.

Chapter 38: Tournaments

Pride FC's tournaments were a hallmark of the organization, showcasing the best fighters in grueling formats that tested endurance, skill, and mental fortitude. These events were highly anticipated by fans and highlighted Pride's ability to gather top-tier competitors from around the world. Each tournament created unforgettable moments, crowning champions who left a permanent mark on mixed martial arts history.

The first tournament was the Pride Grand Prix 2000, an openweight event that featured fighters of all sizes and disciplines. Held across two dates, it culminated in the finals where Mark Coleman of the United States defeated Ukraine's Igor Vovchanchyn. Coleman's victory solidified him as a dominant force, using his superior wrestling and ground-and-pound to become the first Grand Prix champion.

In 2003, Pride held its first middleweight tournament, which saw Brazil's Wanderlei Silva rise to the top. Silva defeated Quinton "Rampage" Jackson in the finals at Pride Final Conflict 2003. His aggressive, high-pressure style was on full display, earning him the tournament victory and further enhancing his reputation as one of the most feared strikers in MMA.

The 2004 heavyweight tournament brought together legends of the sport, including Fedor Emelianenko and Antônio Rodrigo Nogueira. The finals took place during Pride Shockwave 2004, where Emelianenko's tactical brilliance and well-rounded skills allowed him to emerge victorious. This event doubled as a title fight, further cementing Fedor's status as an all-time great.

Pride's 2005 tournaments included two Grand Prix events: the middleweight and lightweight divisions. In the middleweight Grand Prix, Brazil's Mauricio "Shogun" Rua delivered stunning performances to claim victory over compatriot Ricardo Arona in the finals. Meanwhile, in the lightweight division, Takanori Gomi of Japan showcased his exceptional striking and aggression to defeat fellow Japanese fighter Hayato Sakurai, earning the lightweight Grand Prix title at Pride Shockwave 2005.

The welterweight tournament of 2005 ended with Dan Henderson from the United States defeating Brazil's Murilo Bustamante. This tournament also served as a title fight, crowning Henderson as the welterweight champion. Henderson's win underscored his ability to compete in multiple weight classes, further solidifying his legacy as one of the most versatile fighters in Pride history.

In 2006, Pride returned to the openweight format with the Pride Final Conflict Absolute. Croatia's Mirko "Cro Cop" Filipović emerged as the victor, defeating the United States' Josh Barnett in the finals. Filipović's powerful striking and devastating kicks made him a fan favorite and a dominant force in the sport, with this victory becoming one of the defining moments of his career.

The 2006 welterweight Grand Prix featured a diverse roster of fighters, with Japan's Kazuo Misaki taking the top spot. Misaki defeated Canada's Denis Kang in the finals at Pride Bushido 13. This victory was particularly notable as Misaki demonstrated exceptional tactical acumen and endurance, proving that determination and strategy were just as important as raw power.

Each of these tournaments showcased the diversity and depth of talent in Pride FC. They brought together fighters from across the globe, uniting different fighting styles under one roof. Pride's tournaments were not just about crowning champions; they were about creating moments that would forever be etched in the memories of fans. The fighters who competed in these events exemplified the spirit of Pride, making the tournaments a cornerstone of the organization's legacy.

The Grand Finale of Pride Tournaments

The Pride tournaments were much more than just a series of fights; they were a celebration of martial arts at its finest. Each event brought together a mix of legends, up-and-comers, and underdogs, all vying for glory. These tournaments showcased the diversity of fighting styles and the global appeal of mixed martial arts, creating moments that fans would cherish forever.

The openweight tournaments were among the most thrilling. Fighters of different sizes competed on an even playing field, with skill and strategy outweighing sheer physicality. The Pride Grand Prix 2000 set the tone for what would become a signature feature of the organization. Watching Mark Coleman power through the competition showed that even without weight limits, skill could triumph.

As the tournaments expanded into weight divisions, new stars emerged. Wanderlei Silva's dominant performance in the 2003 middleweight Grand Prix highlighted his unmatched ferocity in the ring. His victory was a defining moment, not just for him but for the sport, proving that tournaments could deliver both technical mastery and dramatic finishes.

Heavyweight tournaments brought their own drama. Fedor Emelianenko's victory in 2004 was a testament to his status as the best in the world. His ability to adapt to any opponent, whether standing or on the ground, demonstrated why he remains a legend. The openweight tournaments, like the Pride Final Conflict Absolute in 2006, further emphasized the versatility required to succeed in these grueling competitions.

Lighter divisions also had their share of iconic moments. Takanori Gomi's triumph in the lightweight Grand Prix of 2005 was a masterclass in striking and aggression. Fighters like Dan Henderson, who competed and succeeded across multiple weight classes, became symbols of resilience and adaptability.

The welterweight tournaments often delivered surprises. Kazuo Misaki's victory in 2006 was a story of perseverance and tactical brilliance. His journey to the top showed that a calculated approach could overcome even the toughest competition.

Pride's tournaments didn't just create champions; they told stories. Fighters endured multiple battles in a single night, pushing their physical and mental limits. The format itself was a test of endurance, making every win more meaningful. Fans connected with these warriors, not just for their skills but for their heart and determination.

Looking back, the tournaments remain a shining example of what made Pride special. They celebrated the global nature of martial arts, bringing together competitors from every corner of the world. The fights were unforgettable, and the champions became legends. While Pride may no longer exist, its tournaments live on in the memories of fans and in the history of the sport, inspiring fighters and organizations to this day.

Chapter 39: Notable Fighters

Pride Fighting Championships was home to many of the most skilled, daring, and legendary fighters in mixed martial arts. The athletes who competed in Pride left an indelible mark on the sport, showcasing their abilities on a global stage. Below is an exploration of the most notable fighters in each weight class and their achievements.

Heavyweight Division

Fedor Emelianenko stands out as one of the greatest heavyweights of all time. Undefeated in Pride, he became the last Pride heavyweight champion and won the 2004 Heavyweight Grand Prix. His unmatched composure, technical skill, and resilience made him a near-mythical figure in MMA. Antônio Rodrigo Nogueira was another heavyweight icon. Known for his incredible toughness and submission skills, he was the first Pride heavyweight champion and the runner-up in the 2004 Grand Prix. Mirko "Cro Cop" Filipović brought fear to opponents with his devastating kicks, claiming the 2006 Openweight Grand Prix title.

Mark Coleman, the "Godfather of Ground and Pound," won the 2000 Openweight Grand Prix, solidifying his legacy as an MMA pioneer. Josh Barnett, a submission expert, was a finalist in the 2006 Openweight Grand Prix. Igor Vovchanchyn, a relentless striker, made it to the finals of the 2000 Grand Prix. Ken Shamrock, Kevin Randleman, and Sergei Kharitonov also had memorable moments in Pride, with Randleman and Shamrock bringing UFC championship experience. Mark Hunt, despite his size disadvantage, showcased his striking as a K-1 champion and Pride title challenger. Semmy Schilt, a towering fighter, transitioned from kickboxing to MMA, showing his versatility. Other notables like Don Frye, Kazuyuki Fujita, and Fabrício Werdum contributed significantly to Pride's heavyweight legacy.

Middleweight Division

Wanderlei Silva became synonymous with Pride, reigning as the middleweight champion and winning the 2003 Middleweight Grand Prix. His aggressive style and record-setting accomplishments made him a fan favorite. Mauricio "Shogun" Rua captured the 2005 Grand Prix with dynamic striking and unorthodox techniques. Quinton "Rampage" Jackson, known for his power slams, was a Grand Prix finalist and title challenger.

Kazushi Sakuraba, the "Gracie Hunter," became a legend for defeating members of the famed Gracie family and reaching the 2000 Grand Prix semifinals. Ricardo Arona was a strong contender, reaching the 2005 Grand Prix finals. Fighters like Kiyoshi Tamura, Royce Gracie, Alistair Overeem, and Hidehiko Yoshida brought unique styles to the division. Anderson Silva, who later dominated in the UFC, showcased his striking in Pride, while Murilo Rua, Chuck Liddell, and Vitor Belfort added depth to the middleweight roster.

Welterweight Division

Dan Henderson achieved historic status by becoming the only fighter to hold two Pride belts simultaneously, winning the 2005 Welterweight Grand Prix and the welterweight championship. Kazuo Misaki's 2006 Grand Prix victory highlighted his tactical approach, while Murilo Bustamante reached the 2005 finals. Denis Kang and Paulo Filho were strong contenders, with Filho having to withdraw from the 2006 Grand Prix due to injury.

Ikuhisa Minowa and Akihiro Gono brought unorthodox techniques and grit to the division. Gegard Mousasi, later a champion in other organizations, displayed his versatility in multiple weight classes. Hector Lombard's brief Pride stint showcased his explosiveness, which he later utilized in Bellator.

Lightweight Division

Takanori Gomi was the king of Pride's lightweight division, becoming its only champion and winning the 2005 Grand Prix with a blend of power and precision. Hayato Sakurai, a skilled striker, was the Grand Prix runner-up. Fighters like Marcus Aurélio and Joachim Hansen delivered memorable performances, with Hansen later claiming titles in other promotions.

Luiz Azeredo, Shinya Aoki, Jens Pulver, and Tatsuya Kawajiri represented a mix of striking and grappling excellence. Gilbert Melendez, Daisuke Nakamura, and Nick Diaz further enriched the lightweight roster, with Diaz bringing his trademark toughness and personality.

The Legacy of Pride Fighters

The fighters who competed in Pride not only entertained fans but also elevated the sport of MMA. Their accomplishments in Pride and beyond ensured their places in history. Whether it was Fedor's dominance, Silva's ferocity, or Gomi's explosiveness, these athletes exemplified the best of martial arts. The Pride ring was where legends were made, and these fighters continue to inspire generations of fans and competitors.

A Ring of Legends

The fighters of Pride represent more than just the sport of mixed martial arts—they are legends who carved their stories into the history of combat sports. Each name mentioned in this chapter symbolizes a unique style, journey, and contribution that shaped the identity of Pride and set the foundation for MMA today. From their defining wins to their unforgettable moments, these athletes created a legacy that continues to inspire.

The heavyweights brought unparalleled power and skill to Pride. Fedor Emelianenko's reign showcased what it means to be an unbeaten champion. Mirko "Cro Cop" Filipović's head-kick knockouts remain some of the most replayed moments in MMA history. Antônio Rodrigo Nogueira's legendary toughness and technical mastery gave fans classic battles. Other heavyweights like Mark Coleman and Josh Barnett, with their ground-and-pound and grappling expertise, proved that heavyweights could be both technical and thrilling. These fighters turned the Pride ring into an arena for epic clashes.

The middleweights were no less remarkable. Wanderlei Silva, with his aggressive style, left a trail of chaos and victories in his wake, while Mauricio "Shogun" Rua stunned the world with his dynamic offense. Fighters like Kazushi Sakuraba and Ricardo Arona added technical brilliance and resilience to the mix, creating a division filled with diversity. Each middleweight brought something special, whether it was striking brilliance, submission wizardry, or the ability to entertain.

The welterweights added strategy and finesse to Pride's reputation. Dan Henderson's triumphs in two weight classes demonstrated his versatility and tenacity. Fighters like Kazuo Misaki, Paulo Filho, and Denis Kang kept the division competitive, showing a range of skills from striking to submission grappling. Their performances were tactical and thrilling, creating memorable rivalries and moments.

The lightweights brought speed, precision, and endless energy. Takanori Gomi's dominance in the division proved that smaller fighters could bring as much excitement as the heavyweights. Hayato Sakurai's skill set and others like Marcus Aurélio and Shinya Aoki created battles that were not just fast-paced but also technically brilliant. These fighters reminded fans that MMA was about all dimensions of the sport, from striking to ground game.

Beyond their individual divisions, Pride fighters were trailblazers who influenced the evolution of MMA. They brought fans from around the world into the fold, transcending cultural and national boundaries. Fighters like Nick Diaz, Anderson Silva, and Alistair Overeem went on to achieve greatness elsewhere, proving the depth and quality of Pride's roster.

The Pride ring was more than a stage; it was a crucible where these fighters tested themselves. Their struggles, victories, and defeats were stories told through punches, kicks, and submissions. Every name in this chapter contributed to Pride's legacy as one of the most iconic promotions in MMA history.

While Pride itself may no longer exist, the fighters and their achievements ensure that its spirit lives on. From unforgettable knockouts to legendary rivalries, these warriors made sure that the name "Pride" would forever echo in the world of martial arts. They showed that fighting is more than physical—it's about heart, strategy, and the will to be the best.

Conclusion: The Legacy of Pride FC

Pride Fighting Championships was not just another mixed martial arts organization; it was a phenomenon that forever changed combat sports. From its start in the late 1990s to its final moments in 2007, Pride gave the world some of the most legendary fighters, unforgettable battles, and iconic moments in MMA history. It was an era where warriors stepped into the ring to test their limits, entertain fans, and create a legacy.

At its peak, Pride FC was the gold standard for MMA promotions. Its production value, packed arenas, and dramatic fighter entrances created a spectacle that rivaled anything in combat sports. The massive Tokyo Dome crowds roared with excitement as the world's best fighters squared off in the famous white ring. Fans didn't just witness fights; they experienced stories of triumph, heartbreak, and pure grit. Pride was not just about violence—it was about spirit, respect, and honor.

Pride was the home of legends. Fedor Emelianenko, Wanderlei Silva, Mirko "Cro Cop" Filipović, and Antonio Rodrigo Nogueira became household names, dominating their divisions with skill, toughness, and strategy. Fighters like Kazushi Sakuraba, "The Gracie Hunter," brought an unmatched blend of heart and technique that made him a hero to many. Middleweights, heavyweights, and lightweights alike pushed the boundaries of what people thought was possible in the ring. Each bout felt like a piece of history, and each champion carried the Pride name with pride.

What made Pride unique was its willingness to put on fights fans wanted to see. It didn't matter if someone was undefeated or an underdog—if the matchup was exciting, Pride made it happen. Openweight tournaments and Grand Prix events allowed fighters of all sizes to compete, creating epic battles between athletes from different weight classes. The unpredictability of Pride's events made every fight feel like anything could happen. One strike or one submission could end it all.

The rules of Pride also set it apart. Unlike other MMA promotions, Pride allowed soccer kicks, stomps, and knees to the head of grounded opponents, which gave fighters more weapons to use. These rules created a brutal yet exciting style of fighting that tested the toughness and creativity of the athletes. Pride's fighters had to adapt quickly and be prepared for anything. It was a proving ground for the toughest fighters in the world.

Even after Pride ended, its influence lived on. Many Pride fighters moved to other organizations, such as the UFC, and continued their success. Fighters like Dan Henderson, Mauricio "Shogun" Rua, and Anderson Silva carried the Pride spirit with them, showing the world what Pride veterans were made of. The skills, toughness, and discipline developed in Pride shaped the modern MMA landscape. Pride FC may be gone, but its impact can still be seen in today's fighters and events.

The end of Pride was the end of an era, but its legacy remains strong. Fans still look back fondly at the epic fights, unforgettable moments, and larger-than-life fighters who defined the promotion. Pride created memories that MMA fans will never forget—moments that inspire a new generation of fighters and fans alike. Whether it was Fedor's dominance, Wanderlei's aggression, or Mirko's devastating kicks, Pride's magic is something that will never be recreated.

Pride FC was more than a promotion—it was a movement that brought the art of fighting to life. It combined heart-pounding action with the honor and respect of true martial arts. For fighters and fans alike, Pride was a symbol of what MMA could be at its very best. Though the final bell has long since rung, the spirit of Pride FC will live on forever, reminding us of a time when legends were made, and the world of fighting reached its greatest heights.

The Legacy Lives On

Pride Fighting Championships (Pride FC) was a Japanese mixed martial arts (MMA) organization that operated from 1997 to 2007. During its decade-long run, Pride FC was renowned for its high-quality fights, unique rules, and the assembly of some of the world's best fighters.

Pride FC's events were grand spectacles, often held in large arenas like the Tokyo Dome, attracting tens of thousands of fans. The organization was known for its elaborate fighter entrances, adding a sense of drama and excitement to each event. The use of a boxing-style ring, as opposed to the cage commonly used in other organizations, set Pride FC apart and influenced the dynamics of the fights.

The rules in Pride FC allowed for techniques such as soccer kicks and stomps to the head of a grounded opponent, which were prohibited in other organizations. These rules encouraged a different fighting style and strategy, contributing to the organization's unique identity within the MMA world.

Pride FC was home to many legendary fighters who left an indelible mark on the sport. Fedor Emelianenko, often referred to as "The Last Emperor," remained undefeated in Pride and is considered one of the greatest heavyweights in MMA history. Wanderlei Silva, known as "The Axe Murderer," was the first Pride FC Middleweight Champion and held the record for the most wins, title defenses, and knockouts in Pride history. Other notable fighters included Antônio Rodrigo Nogueira, Mirko "Cro Cop" Filipović, and Kazushi Sakuraba, each contributing to the rich legacy of Pride FC.

The organization was also known for its tournaments, such as the Grand Prix events, which featured fighters from various weight classes competing in a single-elimination format. These tournaments were highly anticipated and showcased some of the most exciting matchups in MMA history.

In 2007, Pride FC was acquired by Zuffa LLC, the parent company of the Ultimate Fighting Championship (UFC). Following the acquisition, many Pride fighters transitioned to the UFC, bringing with them the skills and reputations they had built in Japan. The influence of Pride FC is evident in the evolution of MMA, with many of its fighters achieving success in other organizations and its events serving as a blueprint for modern MMA promotions.

The legacy of Pride FC continues to be celebrated by fans and fighters alike. Its contribution to the global popularity of MMA is undeniable, and its unique approach to the sport has left a lasting impact. The memories of epic battles, legendary fighters, and the electric atmosphere of Pride events remain a cherished part of MMA history.

Pride Fighting Championships played a pivotal role in shaping mixed martial arts into the global phenomenon it is today. Its innovative approach, legendary fighters, and unforgettable events have cemented its place in the annals of combat sports history.

Thank You for Reading This Book

Thank you for taking the time to read *The History of Pride FC*. It has been an incredible journey revisiting the rise, success, and legacy of one of the most influential organizations in mixed martial arts history. Pride Fighting Championships was more than just a fight promotion—it was a movement that changed the sport forever, and I hope this book gave you a deeper appreciation for its impact.

Writing this book has been a labor of love, driven by my admiration for the fighters, the events, and the memories Pride FC created. Whether you're a longtime fan who experienced these moments live or someone discovering Pride for the first time, I hope these pages brought to life the excitement, emotion, and significance of this remarkable organization.

Pride FC introduced the world to legendary fighters who became icons of the sport. Names like Fedor Emelianenko, Wanderlei Silva, Antonio Rodrigo Nogueira, and Kazushi Sakuraba will forever be remembered for their grit, skill, and warrior spirit. These fighters, along with so many others, showed us what true competition looks like and created memories that still resonate with fans worldwide.

As we reflect on Pride FC's legacy, it's impossible to overlook the passion of the fans who made the events so special. The roaring crowds in Japan, the global excitement for Grand Prix tournaments, and the unmatched energy of Pride shows made them unforgettable. This book would not be possible without the fans who have continued to celebrate and share their love for Pride FC over the years.

I also want to thank everyone who has supported me throughout the writing of this book. To those who inspired me, encouraged me, and shared their own memories of Pride FC—thank you. Your stories and enthusiasm reminded me just how important this organization was and continues to be.

For the readers, I hope this book rekindled your passion for the sport and helped you relive some of the greatest moments in MMA history. Pride FC's influence continues to live on in every fighter who steps into the ring or cage, and in every fan who remembers the glory of those epic battles.

As you close this book, I encourage you to keep celebrating the legacy of Pride FC. Watch old fights, share stories with friends, and honor the fighters who gave us their all. The history of Pride is not just about what happened in the past; it's about the way it continues to inspire generations of athletes and fans.

Thank you again for being part of this journey with me. It has been an honor to write this book and share the history of Pride FC with you. The fighters, the moments, and the spirit of Pride will never be forgotten.

If you enjoyed this book, please consider leaving a review by clicking here.

In the spirit of sportsmanship and camaraderie, James Bren.

Other Books by James Bren

The History of MMA

The History of the NFL

The History of the NHL and the Stanley Cup

The History of the UFC – Book 1

111 Weird, Fun, and Random *Facts About the UFC*

The History of the NHL

The History of Bellator

The History of the NBA

The History of Major League Baseball

The History of the UFC – Book 2

The History of Mixed Martial Arts

MMA Manuscripts: 30 Must-Reads in the World of
MMA and Combat Sports

The History of NASCAR

The History of FIFA

The History of the PGA TOUR

The History of the Association of Tennis Professionals

The History of Wimbledon

The History of The National Rugby League

The History of the Indian Premier League

Printed in Great Britain
by Amazon